MANCHESTER
CITY COUNCIL

Please return/renew this item
by the last date shown.
Books may also be renewed by
phone or the internet.

Tel: 0161 254 7777

www.manchester.gov.uk/libraries

To infinity! – A.B.
To ABBC, with love – B.L.
For David & Veronica – S.G.

First published 2021 by Walker Books Ltd
87 Vauxhall Walk, London SE11 5HJ

2 4 6 8 10 9 7 5 3 1

Text © 2021 Alex Bellos and Ben Lyttleton
Illustrations © 2021 Spike Gerrell

The right of Alex Bellos and Ben Lyttleton, and Spike Gerrell
to be identified as authors and illustrator respectively of this work has been
asserted by them in accordance with the Copyright, Designs and Patents Act 1988

This book has been typeset in Gill Sans MT Pro and WB Spike

Printed and bound by CPI Group (UK) Ltd, Croydon CR0 4YY

British Library Cataloguing in Publication Data:
a catalogue record for this book is available from the British Library

ISBN 978-1-4063-8666-0

WALKER
BOOKS

FSC
www.fsc.org
MIX
Paper from
responsible sources
FSC® C020471

www.walker.co.uk
www.footballschool.co

FOOTBALL SCHOOL
TERRIFIC TEAMS

50 TRUE STORIES OF FOOTBALL'S GREATEST SIDES

Alex Bellos & Ben Lyttleton

Illustrated by Spike Gerrell

FOOTBALL SCHOOL

Best of the crest:

The Football School motto is a play on words, in which the English word "kick" is placed in the Latin phrase *cogito ergo sum*, or "I think therefore I am", to mean "I kick, therefore I am".

Kickito Ergo Sum

Mascot:

Ben's dog, Buddy

Home kit:

Pencil, paper, computer

Stadium:

Rotates between bookshops

The team that plays it by the book!

Before we start, we want to introduce you to the most terrific team in the world: Football School! This team features Alex and Ben, but also illustrator Spike, editor Daisy, assistant Maryam, designer Laurelie and, last but not least, you, the reader!

Alex and Ben write their books very much like they play football together. Alex kicks the ball to Ben, who kicks it back to Alex, who kicks it back to Ben, and so on. With books, Alex and Ben are always bouncing ideas back and forth. It is always easier – and more fun! – to get inspiration when you are doing it with a friend.

Once we agree on a subject, we research and write. Alex writes something. Ben writes something. We pass the stories between each other for feedback and comments. There is so much one-two-ing that when the stories are finished you can't tell which started as an Alex story or a Ben story. They have all become Football School stories!

Once the text is done, we show it to Spike. He is an artist of the ball, blessed with amazing technique, sublime creative skills and an enviably large bag of coloured pens. Spike can place a ball in a net with pinpoint accuracy – especially if he is drawing it!

The full list of people involved in making this book a success is a long one, including printers, lorry drivers, salespeople, booksellers – and, of course, readers. It may say Alex and Ben on the cover, but this book is a team effort. We are nothing without our terrific team!

HOME BOYS

Alex and Ben used to live five minutes away from each other. When Ben recently moved house, he made sure his new house was still near to Alex. Now that's a close friendship!

CONTENTS

AC MILAN

Nickname: *I Rossoneri* (The Red and Blacks)

Best of the crest:

The central circle is divided into two. On the left: red and black stripes. The red represents the players' passion and the black their opponents' fear. On the right: the city of Milan flag, a red cross on white.

Mascot:

Milanello the red devil

Home kit:

Red and black striped shirt, white shorts, white socks

Stadium:

San Siro, Milan, cap. 80,000

European giants with an important Legacy

AC Milan are Italy's most successful team in European football. They have won the Champions League – or its predecessor, the European Cup – seven times. Only one team, Real Madrid, has won it more. But the influence of the Rossoneri extends far beyond their trophy cabinet. You red (and black) it here first!

When we see players today pressing opponents close to their own goal, defenders starting high up the pitch and using offside traps, this is all down to the influence of AC Milan. Or more precisely, to one man: Arrigo Sacchi. A tactically brilliant coach, he led AC Milan to successive European Cups in 1989 (which included a 6–1 win over Real Madrid) and 1990.

Sacchi was initially mocked when he was appointed, because he had never played the game professionally, unlike most managers at that time. "I never realized that to be a jockey you had to be a horse first," he replied. Sacchi developed his pioneering tactics after years watching and learning about football, showing that brilliant coaches need not have been top players. "He completely changed how we think about football," said Jürgen Klopp, another great coach who was not a great footballer.

Milan's last European title came in 2007. These days, they are back on the hunt for the top trophies again, inspired by the goals of Franck Kessié and Zlatan Ibrahimović. The Red and Blacks are red and back!

GIGI IN A HURRY

Goalkeeper Gigi Donnarumma was sixteen when he first played for AC Milan in 2015 and seventeen on his Italy debut. He captained AC Milan for the first time aged twenty-one, playing his two-hundredth game.

AL AHLY

Nickname: The Red Devils

Best of the crest:

The eagle has been a symbol of Egypt since the time of the pyramids. The thirteen stars represent nine African Champions League titles, and 40 Egyptian league titles (one star for every ten league titles).

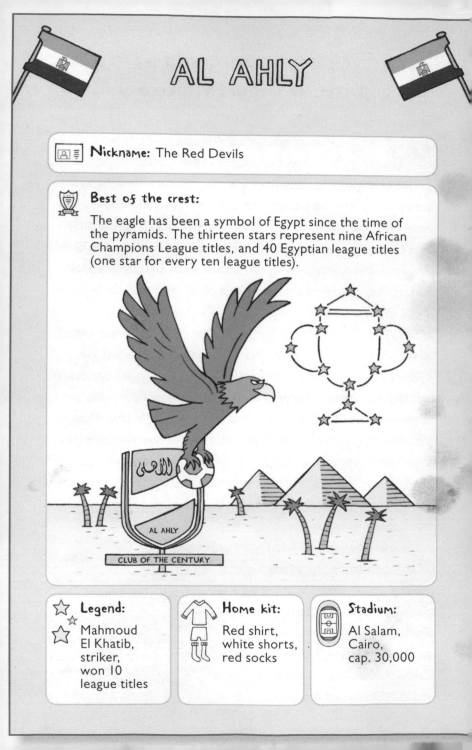

AL AHLY

CLUB OF THE CENTURY

Legend:

Mahmoud El Khatib, striker, won 10 league titles

Home kit:

Red shirt, white shorts, red socks

Stadium:

Al Salam, Cairo, cap. 30,000

Top Egyptian club overcomes tragedy to win African title

When it comes to trophies, Egyptian side Al Ahly are arguably the most successful in the world, having notched up more league titles, cup titles and continental titles than any other major club. Few clubs, however, have experienced tragedy on the scale that they have. In 2012, rival fans attacked Al Ahly fans during an Egyptian league game, causing a riot that left 72 Al Ahly fans dead. It was the greatest disaster in Egyptian football history. Yet it led to the most improbable – and treasured – of all Al Ahly's victories.

Al Ahly are based in Cairo, the capital of Egypt, and are the oldest football club in the country. They have dominated the national league since it began in 1948: there have been 61 seasons so far, and Al Ahly have won 42 of them!

In February 2012, Al Ahly travelled to play Al Masry, a team from Port Said, in a league game. After the match, Al Masry fans ran onto the pitch and attacked Al Ahly players and the visiting fans with bottles, stones and fireworks. It is thought that the violence had little to do with football rivalry, but instead was orchestrated by the Egyptian government as revenge for the involvement of Al Ahly fans in anti-government protests the year before. During the riot, the teams' players fled to the changing room. Fans were crushed in a stampede as they tried to escape the stadium. One fan died in the arms of Al Ahly captain Mohamed Aboutrika.

NATIONAL HEROES

Al Ahly, which means "The National" in Arabic, had their best season in 2005, winning the Egyptian league, Cup, Super Cup, and African Champions League in an unbeaten 46-game run. Unstoppable!

As a result of the tragedy, Egyptian league matches were cancelled. But Al Ahly were also playing in the African Champions League, and they vowed to carry on in the competition. With the trauma and sadness of the tragedy still so fresh, no one expected Al Ahly to be at their best; but the team were desperate to pay tribute to those who had lost their lives.

In the second round, they travelled to Mali and lost 1–0 to Stade Malien. Here again they faced violent scenes, although this time away from the pitch. Straight after the game, a military coup took place – this is when the army seizes power from the government – and there was vicious fighting in the streets. The players were stuck in their hotel for a week as they waited for the chance to get to an airport safely to fly home.

In the second leg against Stade Malien, at home in Cairo, Al Ahly quickly went behind. At half-time, Aboutrika came on. He scored twice to equalize, and then, with two minutes left to play, he volleyed home a glorious winner to send Al Ahly through. The captain had scored a second-half hat-trick!

But the club's challenges were far from over. Al Ahly's coach quit, and Aboutrika was banned for refusing to play in a match where he didn't feel safe. Yet still Al Ahly kept winning.

FINAL
2012
AL AHLY   2 (3)
ESPÉRANCE 1 (2)

In the semi-final, they beat Nigeria's Sunshine Stars 1–0 to reach the final, against Tunisian champions Espérance. The first leg, played in Egypt, finished 1–1. Al Ahly won the second leg 2–1. It was nine months after the Port Said tragedy and the grief was still raw.

Players celebrated wearing shirts with the number 72 on the front, referring to the number of fans who died.

Aboutrika lifted the trophy with a mixture of joy, sadness and pride: joy at their victory, sadness at the lives so tragically lost and immense pride that his team had fulfilled their pledge to honour those lives against all odds.

MOST SUCCESSFUL TEAMS IN THE AFRICAN CHAMPIONS LEAGUE

TEAM	COUNTRY	TITLES	MOST RECENT TITLE
Al Ahly	Egypt	9	2020
Zamalek	Egypt	5	2002
TP Mazembe	DR Congo	5	2015
Espérance ST	Tunisia	4	2019
Hafia FC	Guinea	3	1977
Raja CA	Morocco	3	1999
Canon Yaoundé	Cameroon	3	1980

ALCOYANO

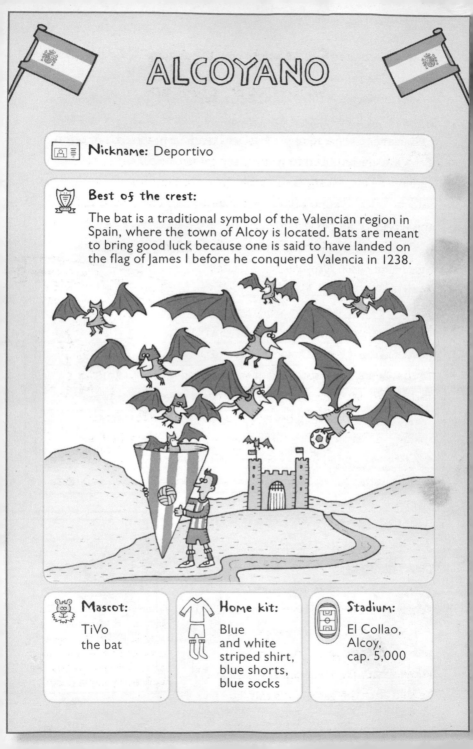

Nickname: Deportivo

Best of the crest:

The bat is a traditional symbol of the Valencian region in Spain, where the town of Alcoy is located. Bats are meant to bring good luck because one is said to have landed on the flag of James I before he conquered Valencia in 1238.

Mascot:

TiVo
the bat

Home kit:

Blue
and white
striped shirt,
blue shorts,
blue socks

Stadium:

El Collao,
Alcoy,
cap. 5,000

Spirited underdogs who never give up

Alcoyano are a semi-professional team from the east of Spain, and are not used to winning big games. In 2021 they caused one of the biggest shocks in Spanish football history when they knocked Real Madrid out of the Spanish Cup. The victory fulfilled the words of an old legend.

There is a well-known phrase used in Spain that goes: *más moral que el Alcoyano*. It translates as "more spirit than Alcoyano" and is used to describe those who have a confidence in winning even if they clearly have no hope. People think it dates back to the 1940s, the last time Alcoyano played in the Spanish first division. That team never gave up!

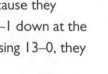

One story has them begging the referee for a few more minutes at the end of a match against Espanyol because they thought they could win – even though they were 7–1 down at the time. Another story claims that when they were losing 13–0, they still felt they could win. That's the Alcoyano spirit!

In 2021, in the Spanish Cup third round, Alcoyano faced Real Madrid, a team packed with international superstars, which cost billions to put together. Alcoyano came from behind to win 2–1. Alcoyano coach Vicente Parras was so proud of his players. "You want to know what *más moral que el Alcoyano* is?" he said after the game. "It's this."

PANDEMIC PAIN

When Alcoyano beat Real Madrid, the town was struggling with the highest coronavirus infection rate in Spain. This was the positive result everyone needed!

AMERICAN SAMOA

Nickname: The Boys from the Territory

Best of the crest:

The crest features the three objects on the table, each of which represents an aspect of Samoan culture: a staff used by the islands' chiefs; the mop-like fue, a symbol of knowledge; and a bowl for kava, a sacred drink.

World Cup record:

Never qualified

Home kit:

Blue and white shirt, blue shorts, blue socks

Stadium:

Pago Park, Pago Pago, cap. 2,000

Dignified in defeat, islanders are the pride of the Pacific

Not all terrific teams win trophies – or even matches. Sometimes losing with your head held high makes a team terrific. And when it comes to terrific losses, no one has lost more terrifically than American Samoa.

This tiny nation is made up of six volcanic islands in the southern Pacific Ocean, and is not to be confused with Samoa, another group of islands about 50 miles away. Samoa is an independent nation, but American Samoa is governed by the US. The two Samoas have many cultural links, but they have many differences too, such as separate currencies and they drive on different sides of the road.

American Samoa's national football team became known across the world when they lost their first ever World Cup qualifier by a world-record margin, and then responded with astonishing dignity. The grim score in their historic defeat against Australia was 31–0!

American Samoa were the lowest-placed team in the FIFA rankings when the match was played in 2001. The odds were stacked against them before kick-off. FIFA had ordered that all players must have American passports to travel to the game in Australia, which took place in a stadium near Brisbane. Nineteen players only had Samoan passports, so were not able to play. Many players from the Under-20 team were ruled out because school exams were taking place at the same time.

 YOU'RE WELCOME!

The population of American Samoa is 55,000. The area produces more NFL players and US servicemen, per head, than any other US territory.

The American Samoa coach cobbled together a group that included three fifteen-year-olds and had an average age of eighteen. Goalkeeper Nicky Salapu was the only first-team player able to make the game – and it was just as well he did!

They were up against an experienced Australia team that included several players from the Premier League. Salapu made a series of impressive saves to keep it goalless after ten minutes. After Con Boutsianis opened the scoring, the deluge began; by half-time it was 16–0; another fifteen goals followed in the second half. Australia striker Archie Thompson ended up scoring a record thirteen goals in the game. American Samoa had only one shot at goal, when they were already 29 goals down. It was saved.

But when the final whistle blew, one team was definitely happiest. They embraced each other and sang with the fans. Can you guess which team it was? American Samoa! They were pleased they had kept the score down, given the players they had, and were grateful to their man-of-the-match, Salapu, who had made over 20 important saves.

But the game haunted him. Fans often reminded him of it and bullies teased his son about the scoreline. Salapu replayed the fixture on the FIFA video game, playing as American Samoa and his son as Australia. To try to get over the defeat, he froze his son's controller (with his permission!) and did not stop playing until American Samoa were winning 50–0.

The impact of the match was long-lasting: FIFA changed their qualifying system so that weaker teams like American Samoa played against opposition of a similar standard in preliminary rounds, to allow them more competitive matches. It meant American Samoa were able to slowly improve and move up the FIFA rankings.

Ten years later, Salapu finally put the loss behind him, when he was part of the American Samoa team that won their first ever match. After a run of 30 successive defeats, American Samoa beat Tonga 2–1 in a World Cup qualifier. Salapu, the only survivor of the 31–0 loss to play, cried tears of joy. He declared, "I'm going to put the past behind me . . . I'm a free man!" After a long, long wait, American Samoa had won at last.

 TERRIFIC TROUNCINGS

These famous games were won by huge margins:

SCORE	COMPETITION	COMMENTS
Arbroath 36 Bon Accord 0	First round of the 1885 Scottish Cup	Largest margin in an honest game of professional football.
AS Adema 149 SO L'Emyrne 0	Madagascan League 2002	Highest score in professional football, but it was a thrown game, in which all the goals were own goals scored in protest.
Hungary 10 El Salvador 1	Group stage of 1982 World Cup	Largest margin in a World Cup match. Even so, Hungary failed to progress beyond the group stage!
USA 13 Thailand 0	Group stage of 2019 Women's World Cup	Largest margin in a Women's World Cup match. USA won the tournament.

ARSENAL

Nickname: The Gunners

Best of the crest:

The cannon reflects the club's name: an arsenal is a place where military weapons are made and stored. The club's founders were employees at Woolwich Arsenal, where weapons were made for the British Army.

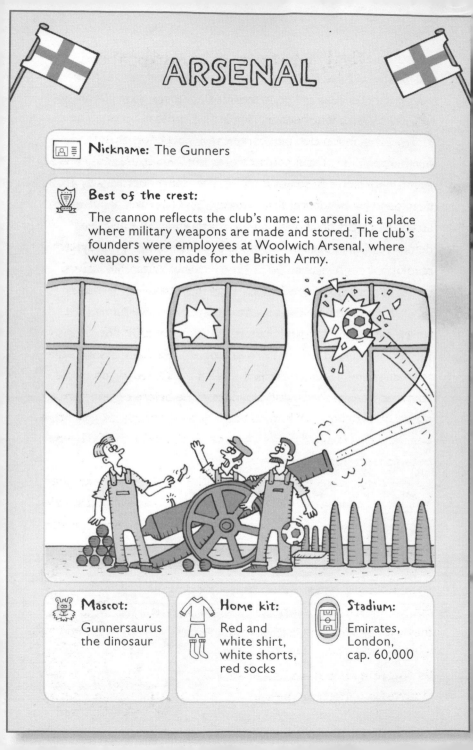

Mascot:
Gunnersaurus the dinosaur

Home kit:
Red and white shirt, white shorts, red socks

Stadium:
Emirates, London, cap. 60,000

Red, white and invincible!

Arsenal have long been making English football history. The north London club pioneered the introduction of shirt numbers in 1933. The first match ever televised by the BBC was Arsenal v. Arsenal Reserves in 1937. That same decade, they developed a new tactical system called "WM", which had five attacking players positioned on the points of a "W", and five defensive players positioned on the points of an "M". The system revolutionised the game. What Magnificence! Wizardly Masters!

When it comes to performance on the pitch, Arsenal have achieved more than most clubs dream of: they have the longest run of any English team without relegation, having been in the top division since 1919. They have won the FA Cup more times than anyone else. And in 2004, the team did something no men's team has done in the English top-flight game before or since: they played 38 matches – 19 home and 19 away – without losing a single one. Let's find out more about the unbeatable team of 2004, who became known to fans as the Invincibles.

The coach at the time was Arsène Wenger, who had won titles in France and Japan before his appointment as Arsenal boss in 1996. When he arrived in London, almost nobody had heard of him, but he quickly won fans over. In his second season, he led the team to victory in the Premier League and FA Cup, and three years later did it again. The double double! But for Wenger this was not good enough. When they won their second league trophy, Arsenal had lost three games. Wenger vowed to win the league again, but in a better way. "I strive for perfection," he said.

Wenger had a knack for putting together teams. He grew up above a pub in France and used to sit in on the local football team's meetings. He once claimed he had been picking teams since he was ten years old! He had long dreamed of going through a season unbeaten, and told his Arsenal players at the beginning of the 2003–4 season that he thought they were the team that could do it. They did not believe him: after all, no one had done it before. It turned out that Wenger knew his team better than they knew themselves!

Wenger's squad had the technical ability to do it. But they needed other things too, like the physical strength to avoid injury. Wenger had changed players' diets and introduced more stretching in training sessions to help make this happen.

They also needed game intelligence and composure under pressure. Wenger was on the case: he encouraged the team to work things out for themselves. He asked them to find the solutions, rather than telling them exactly what to do in every situation. This had a big impact on the players' development and their sense of responsibility in tough games.

Wenger demanded two more things from his team. The first was speed – not just running fast, but also mental speed, so they could make good decisions in a tight game. Winger Robert Pires described Wenger as a chef, adding players from different nations and backgrounds with their own flavours. "Then you mix them and it makes a magnificent dish!"

Finally, the players must have a fierce desire to win. This was enhanced by the players themselves; they became a close group of friends, who would regularly go out for dinners together and discuss tactics.

There were a few times in the season when the task looked beyond them. In their thirty-second game, against Liverpool, Arsenal were 2–1 down at half-time and struggling. But their sense of purpose and drive to win kicked in, and they scored two goals in a minute. The second, a solo goal, was from star striker Thierry Henry with a run that started inside his own half. They ended up winning 4–2.

Once the title victory was sealed, they faced a last-match challenge against Leicester. They were 1–0 down at half-time, but there was no way this team would break their winning streak now! Henry equalized and it was fitting that the team's captain, Patrick Vieira, scored the winning goal. The Invincibles had done it! Another first for this historic English club!

 WHAT A CRAKA!

When Arsenal beat Chelsea 3–1 in the Premier League in December 2020, their scorers were Alexandre Lacazette, Granit Xhaka and Bukayo Saka. Also known as Laca, Xhaka, Saka!

ARSENAL WOMEN

Nickname: The Gunners

Best of the crest:

For almost a century, the cannon on the Arsenal crest pointed left, until in 2002 the club decided to make it point in the other direction. About turn!

Mascot:
Gunnersaurus the dinosaur

Home kit:
Red and white shirt, white shorts, red socks

Stadium:
Meadow Park, Borehamwood, cap. 4,500

The unstoppable team that conquered Europe

The 2004 Arsenal men's team may have been the Invincibles, but around the same time the women's team were even better: they were the Unstoppables. Arsenal Women went unbeaten in the league for four seasons in a row, from 2004–05 to 2007–08, a run that spanned an astonishing 108 games. Talk about gunning for glory!

The high point of the team's history was the 2006–07 season, when they won all six competitions they entered, ending the league campaign with a 100 per cent winning record:

PLAYED	WON	DRAWN	LOST	FOR	AGAINST	POINTS
22	22	0	0	119	10	66

The most prestigious of these six titles was the 2007 UEFA Women's Cup, the forerunner to the Champions League. No one expected Arsenal to win. It was the first – and, as we write this, only – time that an English side has won Europe's top women's tournament.

The final was against Swedish powerhouse Umeå, who had won the title twice before and counted Brazilian superstar Marta in their line-up. Arsenal, on the other hand, had to do without their star player, Kelly Smith, who had been sent off in the semi-final against Brondby (and then been given an extra ban for swearing and kicking over a chair on her way off the pitch).

SMELLY SOCKS ALERT!

Before Arsenal Women turned semi-professional in 2002, many players earned money by working in Arsenal's laundry department. This team knew how to keep a clean sheet!

But this setback made the team even more determined to prove people wrong. In the final minute of the first leg, defender Alex Scott ran up the wing and let fly from 25 yards. Her shot flew into the top of the net to put the Gunners ahead.

Arsenal's 2007 team was full of leaders. They may have been missing Smith, but they could call upon the captains of England (Faye White), Wales (Jayne Ludlow), Scotland (Julie Fleeting) and Ireland (Ciara Grant). In the second leg, the team all worked extra hard to defend their lead. Somehow, Arsenal kept out everything that was thrown at them. At one point, Umeå took a shot that hit the post, cannoned off the goalkeeper's face and hit the post again. But they held on for a 0–0 draw, winning the tie 1–0 on aggregate. Arsenal were champions of Europe!

This victory was a triumphant conclusion to a journey that had started exactly 20 years before. Arsenal Ladies, as they were originally named, were one of the first women's teams set up by a men's football club. In 1987, Vic Akers, a former footballer who worked on Arsenal's community projects, founded the team. Akers went on to coach Arsenal Ladies for 21 years in addition to his other jobs at Arsenal, which included being the kit-man for the men's first team. (He used to sit next to Arsène Wenger in the dugout during Arsenal games, always wearing shorts, whatever the weather.)

Even though they had the name of a big club, Arsenal Ladies started off as an amateur team, meaning that the players were not paid. Many of them had other full-time jobs. Sometimes training started at nine o'clock in the evening so players could get there on time.

Arsenal Ladies won their first league title in 1992 and more than 30 trophies followed during Akers' years in charge. They are the most successful women's team in English football history, winning nine straight league titles between 2003 and 2012.

Now known as Arsenal Women, the team helped usher in a new era of women's football, which over the last decade and a half has become fully professional. The team are still winning league titles, most recently in 2019, thanks to the goals of Dutch phenomenon Vivianne Miedema, one of the game's biggest stars. These hotshot gunners are still aiming high!

QUEEN KELLY

Kelly Smith played for Arsenal over three different periods. A forward who has been described as England's best ever player – she once scored from the halfway line against Russia in Euro 2009 – she retired in 2017 and is now an ambassador for women's football. Altogether, she helped Arsenal win four league titles and three FA Cups. She also inspired a generation of players, like Arsenal stars Jordan Nobbs and Leah Williamson, to work hard and follow their dreams.

ATHLETIC BILBAO

Nickname: *Los Leones* (The Lions)

Best of the crest:

The bridge and church are Bilbao landmarks. The oak tree represents the freedom of the Basque people. The two wolves and the X-shaped crosses are from the crest of the Haro family, who founded the city.

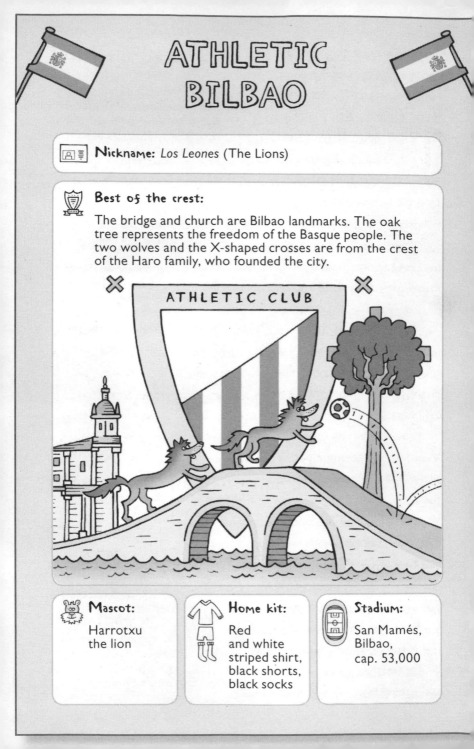

Mascot:
Harrotxu the lion

Home kit:
Red and white striped shirt, black shorts, black socks

Stadium:
San Mamés, Bilbao, cap. 53,000

Spanish winners who Basque in glory

The biggest clubs tend to sign the best players, wherever they come from. What makes Spanish club Athletic Bilbao unique is that they only pick players from their local region, a talent pool of three million people. (Spain has a total population of 47 million people.) You might expect this policy to put Athletic at a huge disadvantage, but that doesn't seem to be the case. They are one of the country's most successful clubs, one of only three (the others being Real Madrid and Barcelona) never to have been relegated from La Liga, the top division.

The region of Spain around Bilbao is called the Basque Country, and the people who live there are called Basques. The Basques have different traditions to the Spanish. Many of them speak Basque, a language that is not related to any other in the world. Since 1912, Athletic has only picked Basque players. In Bilbao, success is local!

There are advantages to Athletic's "grow-your-own" approach. For example, everyone who grows up in the Basque Country supports the club, which means that their first-team players have been fans all their lives. Athletic players are prepared to give everything to their team, because the team represents who they are as people. "Athletic Club is more than a football club, it is a feeling," explained one former club president. "We see ourselves as unique in world football and that defines our identity." No wonder Athletic supporters are among the most passionate in Spain!

SAINTLY GUIDANCE

Athletic Bilbao (and Atlético Madrid) wear the red and white vertical stripes of Southampton FC, after a Bilbao student in 1909 brought home 50 Saints shirts from England.

The image that the Basques have of themselves is of a people used to working hard, respecting others and collaborating in a team. These qualities are reflected in the way Athletic plays. There are also practical reasons why it makes sense to attract, and keep hold of, local talent. Most of the new players in the team are promoted from the youth academy and so are used to the club, the players, the coach and the style of play. Their best signings are usually those they already have!

Athletic have had plenty to cheer over the years. Only Real Madrid and Barcelona have won more trophies in Spanish football history. The last of their eight league titles came in 1984 and in 2015 they won the Spanish Super Cup after beating Barcelona 5–1 over two matches. Over 50,000 fans spilled out onto the streets to celebrate that win.

In 2021, they won the trophy again: this time beating Barcelona 3–2 in a dramatic come-from-behind victory. (Sadly, the streets were empty after that success due to coronavirus pandemic restrictions.)

The other advantage that Athletic have over their rivals is the ability to keep players at the club for a long time. The reason for this is twofold: one, Athletic players are more emotionally connected to their club, so in less of a hurry to leave; and two, because Athletic don't spend huge sums on buying players, they can afford to pay their players a hefty salary. If a rival club want to buy an Athletic player, they have to pay an expensive transfer fee. Manchester City paid Athletic nearly £60 million for defender Aymeric Laporte in 2017 while, one year later, Chelsea paid over £70 million for goalkeeper Kepa Arrizabelaga.

Athletic spent those funds on improving the youth academy to develop the next generation of players, rather than risking the money on a new signing who may or may not play well. From a business point of view, Athletic is one of the best-run clubs in the world.

Athletic fans are proud of their unique approach to football. They say they would rather be relegated with their team of locals than win more trophies with players from across the world. The team are connected to their city more than any other. Everyone knows someone at the club and everyone is a supporter. If football is about creating a community and a sense of belonging, then Athletic Bilbao are true champions!

AUSTRALIA WOMEN

Nickname: The Matildas

Best of the crest:

The crest is an image of Australia's coat of arms. The kangaroo and the emu represent progress since they both find it hard to walk backwards. They are holding a shield with the badges of the six Australian states.

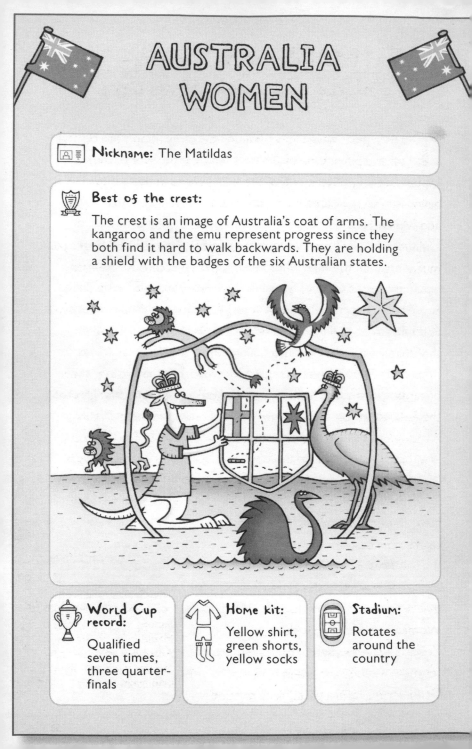

World Cup record:

Qualified seven times, three quarter-finals

Home kit:

Yellow shirt, green shorts, yellow socks

Stadium:

Rotates around the country

Matildas waltz to the World Cup with equal pay

The Matildas have shown grit and determination both on and off the pitch. One of the best teams in the world, they are captained by Sam Kerr, one of the best players in the world. They have also made a name for themselves by fighting for their rights – and winning!

In Australia, women who played for the Matildas used to get paid much less than the men who played for the Socceroos, the men's national team. They also trained at worse facilities. In 2015, shortly after the Matildas reached the World Cup quarter-finals, their best finish, the Australian football federation arranged two friendlies in the USA against the USA national team.

But the Matildas refused to go. They went on strike. Yes, they became a team of strikers – even the goalkeeper! The Matildas told the federation that they needed more money and better facilities if they were going to represent Australia abroad. Quite right too! Negotiations took a long time, but finally, in 2019, the Australian federation agreed that the Matildas would get the same deal as the Socceroos. (Norway, New Zealand, England and Brazil are other countries whose men's and women's teams now earn the same.)

The Matildas scored another victory shortly afterwards, when FIFA announced that Australia would co-host the 2023 Women's World Cup with New Zealand. Australia wants to use the tournament to shape a better world. Gender equality is a great place to start!

IN THE BAG!

The Matildas' nickname comes from Australia's most famous song, "Waltzing Matilda". The phrase is old Australian slang, meaning "to travel with all one's belongings in a bag".

BARCELONA

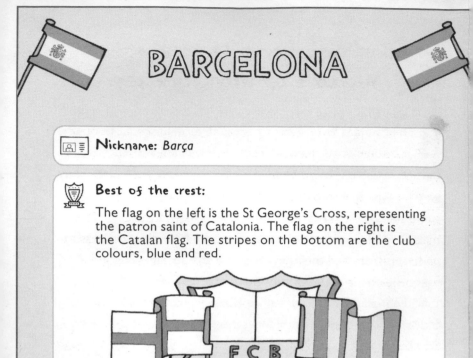

Nickname: *Barça*

Best of the crest:

The flag on the left is the St George's Cross, representing the patron saint of Catalonia. The flag on the right is the Catalan flag. The stripes on the bottom are the club colours, blue and red.

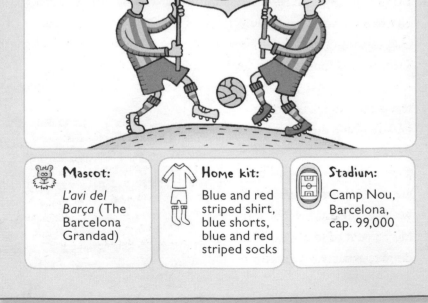

Mascot:

L'avi del Barça (The Barcelona Grandad)

Home kit:

Blue and red striped shirt, blue shorts, blue and red striped socks

Stadium:

Camp Nou, Barcelona, cap. 99,000

Trophies, glory and the most remarkable comeback in history

Barcelona are loved across the world for their beautiful football. Since star player Lionel Messi made his debut in 2004, they have won more than 30 trophies. In one amazing year, 2009, they were crowned champions of Spain, Europe and the world! One game stands out as representing the very best of the club. This match did not win them a trophy, but it showed their composure under pressure and their never-say-die attitude. It reminded everyone of the magic of football.

In February 2017, Paris Saint-Germain beat Barcelona 4–0 in the first leg of a last-sixteen Champions League tie. It seemed that Barcelona were as good as out. No team in the previous 62 years of European knockout competitions had ever gone on to win from such a deficit. But true champions never give up.

The second leg, at Barcelona's Camp Nou, took place the following month. Brazilian forward Neymar was playing for Barcelona at the time. He said his team only had a one per cent chance of qualifying. But even that small chance convinced his team-mates that they might still be able to win. Barcelona coach Luis Enrique was actually confident before the game. He asked the players if they had ever been involved in a *remontada*, the Spanish word for "comeback", before. Most said no, but the belief in the dressing room was growing.

INCREDIB-LEO

Lionel Messi scored for Barcelona in 21 league games in a row, and he scored more than 40 goals a year for ten years running. A dazzling decade!

That was reflected on the pitch. Barcelona's Luis Suárez opened the scoring after five minutes. PSG looked nervous. They had so many players marking Messi that there was plenty of room for Neymar to cause havoc. Just before half-time, Neymar's cross was turned in for another goal. Barcelona were 2–0 up (although 4–2 down on aggregate). The Camp Nou fans were chanting, *"Si, se puede!"* – "Yes, we can!"

At half-time, Luis Enrique told his players to stay calm. "Boys, even if there are only five minutes left, you'll still be able to score three goals," he said. Five minutes after the break, Messi scored a penalty and it was 3–0. Barcelona were almost there!

Perhaps they got complacent, or thought the job was already done. They relaxed. And PSG made them pay. Soon after hitting the post, Edinson Cavani scored a crucial away goal for PSG. Barcelona would now need three more goals to win the tie. (In European matches, when the two-legged score is level, away goals count as double, so Cavani's goal meant that a 5–1 win for Barcelona would still not be enough.)

With just 30 minutes left on the clock, even Neymar started to think this might be beyond Barcelona. PSG squandered two more chances. Suddenly there were only five minutes left. Still, three goals required. But the players knew what the coach had said. It was still possible.

After 88 minutes, Neymar curled a free kick from outside the area into the top corner. The score was now 4–1. Barcelona needed two more goals. One minute later, Suárez fell in the box and won a penalty. Neymar scored again. 5–1. One more goal needed. And now the game was in injury time. *"Si, se puede!"* cheered the fans.

Barcelona won another free kick. This time Neymar's effort was cleared. But instead of firing it back into the area, he jinked around one opponent, dodged past another and floated the perfect cross into the area. It fell to Sergi Roberto, who headed the ball into the net to make it 6–1. The *remontada* was complete! Incredible scenes of jubilation followed. The players – from both teams – couldn't believe what had just happened!

Barcelona did not go on to win the Champions League that year. In fact, they were knocked out in the next round by Juventus. PSG responded to their defeat by buying Neymar for £200 million, making him the most expensive signing in the history of football. That was partly down to his performance that day.

Despite that incredible game, Barcelona no longer dominate European football as they once did. Their era of success – between 2005 and 2019, they won ten league titles, four Champions League finals and three Club World Cups – has (for the moment at least) come to an end. But sometimes, even for the biggest clubs in the world, one magical, crazy, once-in-a-lifetime performance can have more impact than a run-of-the-mill victory. We remember this *remontada* because it seemed so unlikely. Barcelona taught us to believe that nothing is impossible – although it helps if you have Neymar on your team!

BAYERN MUNICH

Nickname: *Die Roten* (The Reds)

Best of the crest:

Bayern is the German name for Bavaria, which was a kingdom until 1918 and is now a state in Germany. Munich is the capital of Bavaria. The criss-cross pattern of blue and white diamonds is taken from the Bavarian flag.

Mascot:
Berni the bear

Home kit:
Red shirt, red shorts, red socks

Stadium:
Allianz Arena, Munich, cap. 75,000

Brilliant Bayern are one big football family

Bayern Munich are the marvellous monarchs of German football. They are the most successful club in the country and their recipe for success is not about paying big amounts for talent, but about keeping hold of their best players, even when they retire. When you join Bayern, it's for life!

Bayern are known for being smart with money. For example, Bayern consistently buy their opponents' best players. The effect is doubled: it not only strengthens their own team but also weakens the others. Crafty! Between 2013 and 2020, they won a record eight Bundesligas in a row, and have three Champions League victories to add to their three European Cups.

You can imagine how well this goes down with fans of other clubs, and there are plenty of fans in Germany who don't like Bayern Munich. Yet even Bayern's enemies will grudgingly admit the club has done great things for German football, such as developing players for the national team and digging into their pockets to help other teams in need. When rival clubs like St Pauli and Borussia Dortmund were in crisis, they gave them financial support.

Bayern also heavily invest in youth, which means that their squad is assembled relatively cheaply compared to the other European giants. For example,

KING COMAN!

When Bayern's French winger Kingsley Coman scored the winning goal against his old club, PSG, in the 2020 Champions League final, he became the first player in the history of the competition to score against a former club in the final. Awkward!

the combined transfer value of Bayern's starting eleven against Paris Saint-Germain in the 2020 Champions League final came to a total of €105 million, which was less than half the amount PSG had paid to sign Brazilian star Neymar.

When Bayern beat Paris Saint-Germain 1–0 and took the 2020 Champions League title, they set a new record: it was the first time a team had won all eleven of their matches in the competition. In some cases, they absolutely destroyed their opposition: they beat Red Star Belgrade 6–0, Spurs 7–2, Chelsea 4–1 and Barcelona 8–2 on their way to the final. This Bayern were baying for blood!

Coach Hansi Flick had been appointed mid-season after a poor start to the campaign. A former midfielder for Bayern (yes, they like to appoint their own!), he won over the players by listening to them. He let them play in the attacking formation they loved. After two early defeats in his reign, Bayern became unbeatable – they won 25 and drew one of their remaining 26 games that season.

The 2020 Bayern squad was made up of older players like Manuel Neuer, Thomas Müller and Jérôme Boateng, who last won the Champions League back in 2013. There were also younger stars including Serge Gnabry, Joshua Kimmich and Alphonso Davies, who were chasing their first big title. The two groups bonded over their shared ambition. "We are a crazy bunch of guys, always willing to help each other out, with incredible togetherness," said Müller after the final.

Bayern's 2020 win put them back at the top of European football, a position they'd first occupied in the mid-1970s with three European Cups (the forerunner to the Champions League) in a row. Bayern beat Atlético Madrid (1974), Leeds United (1975) and Saint-Étienne (1976) in the European Cup finals to secure their place in European football history.

The key players in that successful team, including Franz Beckenbauer and Uli Hoeness, also helped West Germany win the 1974 World Cup. Beckenbauer and Hoeness went on to work for Bayern as directors and board members, masterminding a club ethos and strategy that has maintained the club's position as one of the most admired in Europe.

The tradition of former players running the club continues to this day. Oliver Kahn, a goalkeeper who won the 2002 Champions League with Bayern, is on the board, and in 2022 he is due to take on the role of CEO, the club's highest-ranked executive. When he decides to stop playing, Müller is expected to be next to move from the changing room to the boardroom. This is the Bayern way!

Cheers!

CHEERS!

Munich is famous for its Oktoberfest. The whole city, including Bayern's players, wear traditional Bavarian dress, including lederhosen (leather shorts with braces), and drink beer.

BRAZIL

Nickname: *A Seleção* (The Selection)

Best of the crest:

The initials CBF stand for Confederação Brasileira de Futebol, or Brazilian Football Confederation. The white cross is a type of Christian cross used by medieval knights and popular with the Portuguese, who were the first Europeans to arrive in the region that later became Brazil.

World Cup record:

Winners 1958, 1962, 1970, 1994 and 2002

Home kit:

Yellow shirts, blue shorts, white socks

Stadium:

Rotates around the country

Multi-racial, multi-winning champions of the beautiful game

Whenever the Brazilian national team runs onto the pitch, every football fan in the world feels a thrill of excitement. The vivid yellow of Brazil's shirts embodies the team's flamboyance, the dazzling skills of the players and the shine of their many trophies. Not only have Brazil won five World Cups – more than anyone else – but they have done so playing a type of playful, attacking football that has become known as the "beautiful game". Brazilliant Brazil!

Brazil is a factory for producing players with amazing technique: Neymar for his flicks, Roberto Firmino for his dribbles, Philippe Coutinho for his free kicks and Gabriel Jesus for his finishing. Yet these current players are just the latest on a conveyor belt that has been running for more than 80 years. Indeed, the first member of the Brazil national team to become a sensation in Europe was striker Leônidas da Silva, who wowed crowds at the 1938 World Cup in France. He was voted the tournament's best player and was its top scorer. He performed the first bicycle kick seen in Europe and even scored one goal barefoot when his boot got stuck in the mud!

Since then, nimble-footed legends like Pelé, Romário, Ronaldo, Kaká and Ronaldinho have all become World Cup champions for Brazil. Yet Brazil's success is not only down to fancy tricks and technical skills. Champions need proper preparation, and Brazil takes its World Cups very, very seriously.

FINDERS KEEPERS!

Brazil are famous for their attackers, yet in recent seasons Manchester City and Liverpool have both won the Premier League with Brazilian goalkeepers. Glove-ly!

It is no exaggeration to say that football is more important to Brazilians than it is to the inhabitants of any other country. Brazil is one of the most racially diverse countries in the world, and a century ago, Brazilians saw their diversity as a weakness. But when their football team – which included white, Black and mixed-race players – began to achieve international success, Brazilians of all colours changed their minds. They realized diversity was a great strength! Football is what made Brazilians proud to be Brazilians.

Brazil were so desperate to win the 1958 World Cup in Sweden that the team hired a psychologist, making them one of the first national teams to do so. They also included a dentist in their entourage. Such care was taken to focus on the football that the Brazil team doctor asked the members of a nudist camp visible from the windows of the team hotel if they could wear clothes – he didn't want his players distracted!

Brazil won in 1958. That team, which starred a seventeen-year-old Pelé, played in an attacking, dynamic, irrepressible way that was to become Brazil's trademark. Brazil won again in 1962 and for a third time in 1970. In the 1970 final, a 4–1 victory over Italy, Brazil scored one of the most memorable World Cup goals: six outfield players passed the ball before the seventh, Pelé, laid on a perfect short pass to the eighth, captain Carlos Alberto, who thundered it home from the edge of the box. It was a stunning showcase of how Brazil's individually brilliant footballers could work together perfectly as a team.

Brazil's fourth and fifth World Cup victories came in 1994 and 2002. Their fortunes have dipped since then. Their lowest moment was a 7–1 defeat against Germany in the 2014 World Cup semi-final, which took place in Brazil. The defeat – which ended a 62-match unbeaten streak in competitive matches at home – was a national humiliation. Most countries dream of appearing in a World Cup semi-final. But for Brazil, the 2014 semi-final was one of the greatest disasters in their country's sporting history.

Brazil is the only country to have taken part in every World Cup. The team will surely qualify for the next one and the one after that. They will probably be the favourites to win both of them. With a seemingly endless supply of world-class players, only a fool would bet against the team snatching the trophy back in the future. Go Brazzziiiiiil!

BUNGAY TOWN

Nickname: The Black Dogs

Best of the crest:

The terrifying hound is Black Shuck, a ghost dog who, according to folklore, visits churchyards and attacks people. In 1577, Shuck is said to have appeared after lightning struck Bungay's church.

BUNGAY TOWN CLUB

Legend:
Craig Hunting, defender, played 566 games

Home kit:
Blue shirt, black shorts, black socks

Stadium:
Maltings Meadow, Bungay, cap. 2,000

The team where everyone had the same name

Some teams are terrific because of their results and some because of their ideas. For Bungay Town, an amateur team from Bungay, Suffolk, who play in the Anglian Combination league, it's certainly the latter. They hosted a match unlike any played before.

The game in question was a commentator's dream. There was no danger of forgetting the name of any goalscorer, because every player on the pitch had the same surname: Bungay!

The idea for a match between 22 players called Bungay came from one of the club's fans, Shaun Cole, who wanted to make Bungay Town famous – and raise some money for charity at the same time. He got in touch with Bil Bungay, an advertising expert based in London, and they came up with the idea to find enough people with the surname Bungay for a match. It is a rare name, with only a few hundred Bungays living in the UK. (In fact, everyone called Bungay is the descendent of someone who used to live in the town.) Together they used social media to reach out to Bungays from all over the world. More than 60 of them came to the match, which took place in 2012.

They came from far and wide. Joe Bungay flew in from the USA, while goalkeeper Chris Bungay travelled all the way from Australia. That's a long way to come – especially as his match was cut short when he was sent off for throwing his gloves at the referee.

TERRIFIC TOWN

A Suffolk club has only once been English champions. Ipswich Town won the First Division, the top tier at the time, in 1962.

The Bungay bonanza was not limited to the players. The referee was John Bungay, a qualified official from Hampshire, the mascot was eight-year-old Carla Bungay, and Dr Elizabeth Bungay was the match medic in case of injuries.

On the pitch, the teams were evenly matched, and not just in their names. The game finished 6–6.

Cole, who is now club chairman, continues to come up with schemes to keep the club in the spotlight. He once doubled the crowd by paying every fan 5p to watch a match. Cheered on by all those supporters, the team won 11–0. For another match, he gave a free box of mushrooms to every fan. We're not sure if there was much room for everyone that day!

We salute Cole and how his crackpot ideas have helped his team. He has put brilliant Bungay well and truly on the map. What a fun-gi, and a great spore-t!

 DA SILVA LININGS

There are only a few hundred Bungays in the UK, which makes it a relatively rare surname. In fact, for every Bungay, there are about 2,000 people called Smith, the most common surname in the UK. Here are the most common surnames in some different countries:

SURNAME	COUNTRY	NUMBER OF PEOPLE
Wang	China	107 million
Devi	India	70 million
Da Silva	Brazil	20 million
Kim	South Korea	11 million
Ibrahim	Nigeria	3.2 million
Smith	USA	3 million
Garcia	Spain	1.5 million
Smith	UK	750,000
Müller	Germany	700,000

CAMEROON

Best of the crest:

The Cameroon crest traditionally features a lion, an animal native to the country but now endangered there.

World Cup record:

7 appearances, 1990 quarter-final

Home kit:

Green shirt, red shorts, yellow socks

Stadium:

Ahmadou-Ahidjo, Yaoundé, cap. 40,000

African trailblazers who caused biggest World Cup shock

Cameroon are the kings of African football. They have qualified for the World Cup more times than any other team in the continent, they have won the Africa Cup of Nations more times than any other team south of the Sahara, and their under-23s won the Olympic gold medal in 2000. Everyone trembles when these Lions roar!

Cameroon are also the team that made the world take African football seriously. It is now common to see African players – like Sadio Mané, Riyad Mahrez and Hakim Ziyech – in the world's best clubs, and African national teams regularly beat European and South American ones. But this has only happened in the last 30 years. In the decades before that, African teams lacked facilities and access to the best coaching ideas and, as a consequence, were easily defeated by the world's top football nations.

So when Cameroon played Argentina in the opening game of the 1990 World Cup, no one expected Cameroon to trouble the 1986 World Cup winners. The odds were against them: Argentina had the world's best player, Diego Maradona, in their team, while Cameroon's coach was a Russian who spoke neither English or French (the country's two main languages). The Lions had lost all their pre-tournament preparation matches, most of their squad played in the under-funded

GIANT LEAPS

Cameroon is home to the world's biggest species of frog, the goliath bullfrog, which can grow wider than a football and weigh more than three kilograms.

Cameroon league and the players were upset because the country's president had demanded that a 38-year-old striker who had retired three years earlier be part of the squad.

However, Cameroon's organisation, determination and some vicious tackling resulted in the biggest shock in modern World Cup history: a 1–0 victory against Argentina, the title holders. Cameroon had two players sent off but, despite playing with only nine men, still deserved to beat Maradona's stunned (and bruised) team.

Their next game, against Romania, proved the Argentina result was no fluke. The coach brought on that old striker, Roger Milla, in the second half. Fifteen minutes from time, with the game goalless, Milla shrugged off his marker and scored. He was the oldest scorer in World Cup history!

He set off to the corner flag and danced in front of it, wiggling his hips with a big smile on his face. Ten minutes later, he scored a second time, and danced again. Not only had Milla sent Cameroon into the next round, he had invented a new way of celebrating goals!

Colombia was next up, in Cameroon's first ever World Cup knockout tie. Again, Milla came on as a substitute. The score was 0–0 after 90 minutes, so the match went into extra time. Milla scored within five minutes of coming on. Two minutes later, he tackled the Colombian goalkeeper on the edge of the area and rolled the ball into an empty net. Another goal and another hip-wiggling celebration! The final score was 2–0. Cameroon were in the World Cup quarter-finals and Milla was sending the whole world wiggly with his goals and dancing!

No African team had come this far before. England were next up. England took a first-half lead, but Cameroon hit back and went ahead in the second half. A late penalty from Gary Lineker made it 2–2 and the game went into extra time, during which Lineker scored another penalty. England made it to the semi-finals, but only just. The Indomitable Lions had missed out – by a whisker!

Their performances in the tournament had surprised everyone and redefined the image of African football around the world. Africa was now a force to be reckoned with. Milla thinks Cameroon would have won the World Cup if they had got past England, but we will never know. Four years later, Milla broke his own record as the World Cup's oldest goalscorer, scoring against Russia at the age of 42. This Roger wasn't such an old codger!

We are still waiting for an African team to go further than Cameroon did in 1990. Senegal (in 2002) and Ghana (in 2010) also reached the quarter-finals. It is surely only a matter of time before an African team win the World Cup and, when they do, they will thank Cameroon for leading the way.

 TOP THOMAS

Cameroon goalkeeper Thomas N'Kono's performances at the 1990 World Cup inspired a twelve-year-old Italian boy to change his position and become a goalkeeper. That boy was Gigi Buffon, who became Italy's greatest ever No 1, winning the 2006 World Cup. He even gave his son the middle name Thomas, after N'Kono. The two goalkeepers are now great friends.

CHELSEA

Nickname: The Blues

Best of the crest:

The lion is holding a crozier, a hooked staff used by a bishop, which is a reference to nearby Westminster Abbey.

Mascot:

Stamford the lion

Home kit:

Blue shirt, blue shorts, white socks

Stadium:

Stamford Bridge, London, cap. 41,000

The club where coaches are always watching their jobs!

There's one question every new Chelsea coach has to ask when they get appointed: will I have time to unpack my suitcase? Since super-rich owner Roman Abramovich bought the club in 2003, no Premier League team has made more managerial changes, with seventeen different appointments in the last eighteen years. This Chelsea likes to chop and change!

The strategy seems to work. Chelsea won five Premier League titles, five FA Cups and three European trophies in the same period. But as soon as results take a downturn, the coach can expect to get the chop. Get that suitcase packed again!

In 2012, Chelsea won the Champions League final (for the first time) with a temporary coach, Roberto di Matteo, in charge. He kept the job after the final – but not for long!

In 2017, they hired an Italian coach, Antonio Conte, who had never coached in England before. After six games in charge, he changed the team tactics, picking only three defenders – normally Cesar Azpilicueta, David Luiz and Gary Cahill – in a 3-4-3 formation.

The team went on to win a record-breaking thirteen matches in a row and they ended the season by winning the Premier League. It was the first time any English team had won the title with only three defenders. Three-sy does it!

Conte left one year later. That's life on Chelsea's coaching merry-go-round. All aboard!

WELL, FRANKLY...

Chelsea's all-time leading goalscorer is English midfielder Frank Lampard, with 211 goals. He was appointed Chelsea coach in 2019 – and sacked eighteen months later. Harsh!

CHELSEA WOMEN

Nickname: The Blues

Best of the crest:

The lion originally comes from the coat of arms of the Cadogan family, which owns lots of land in the London neighbourhood of Chelsea.

Mascot:

Bridget the lioness

Home kit:

Blue shirt, blue shorts, white socks

Stadium:

Kingsmeadow, Kingston upon Thames, cap. 5,000

The wise woman and the team that kept their heads

In contrast to the coaching merry-go-round at the Chelsea men's team, the guiding principle at the Chelsea women's squad is stability. Coach Emma Hayes took charge in 2012, when the team were at the bottom of the table, and has built them up to be strong enough to challenge for the Champions League. She holds the records for the most matches managed in the Women's Super League and for the most titles won. Oh my Hayes!

Hayes has an unconventional background for a top football coach. Before she decided that she wanted to work in sport, she trained with the army to be a spy! This might explain why, in her football career, she has displayed a brilliant strategic mind, the military skills of discipline and organisation and a great ability to get the best out of her players. This international woman of mystery has a licence to coach!

Hayes is from England, but moved to the USA at the age of 25 to begin her coaching career. She started off at a boys' Under-10 team and moved on to older levels, eventually coaching semi-professional women's teams. She moved back to the UK in 2006 to be assistant coach at Arsenal, and was part of the squad during their most successful season in 2007.

When she took the Chelsea job in 2012, the team were not very terrific. Chelsea had never won a trophy in their history. That almost changed on the final day of the 2014 season, when Chelsea needed to beat Manchester City to clinch their first ever league title. But they lost 2–1, allowing Liverpool to snatch the title on goal difference. The Blues had the blues!

The next season, they had another chance at glory. Chelsea faced Notts County in the 2015 FA Cup final. On the morning of the game, Hayes did something quite unlike any other coach. She cut pink roses from her garden and presented one to each player, together with an inspirational poem. She said: "My young players were like, 'The gaffer's off her head', but my senior players were like, 'What a lovely gesture'. I grew the flowers in my garden, that was my gift to them, and their gift to me was what they did."

The verse did the trick. Poetry in motion! Chelsea won 1–0 and the trophy was theirs.

POETRY CORNER

The poem that Emma Hayes gave to her players was "If", by Rudyard Kipling. It was written around 1895 and is a bit like a self-help guide to becoming a better person. Its famous first lines are:

If you can keep your head when all about you
Are losing theirs and blaming it on you,
If you can trust yourself when all men doubt you,
But make allowance for their doubting too;

Its last lines are:

If you can fill the unforgiving minute
With sixty seconds' worth of distance run,
Yours is the Earth and everything that's in it,
And—which is more— you'll be a Man, my son!

But Hayes changed the words of the last line to:

And—which is more—you'll be a wise woman!

She is a wise woman indeed!

The team went on to win their first league title in the same season. Hayes was slowly building a dynasty at the club, as Chelsea finished in the top two for eight seasons in a row. They went even better in 2020, when the team was controversially awarded the title after the coronavirus pandemic ended the season early. Chelsea had fewer points than Manchester City, but had played fewer games so were handed the title on a points-per-game basis.

MUST TRY, HARDER

Chelsea broke the world transfer record signing striker Pernille Harder for the 2021 season, the same year she was voted the world's best female player. She's faster, stronger and Harder than the rest!

Hayes has turned Chelsea into one of England's top women's teams. Now her target is to do the same in Europe. Chelsea reached the Champions League semi-finals in 2018 and 2019, but Hayes is determined to improve on that and become the continent's best.

Hayes is often suggested for other coaching jobs when they become vacant. In fact, she is tipped to be the first female head coach to take charge of a high-level men's team in the UK. Not that she is in any rush. She doesn't like the idea that the women's game might be seen as a stepping-stone to the men's game. She says there is no need to switch when she can work with some of the world's best players, such as Sam Kerr, Bethany England and Pernille Harder, at Chelsea. And she's quite right!

CORINTHIAN

Nickname: The Corinthians

Best of the crest:

The club's name derives from the ancient Greek city of Corinth, which also gives its name to the section of the Bible called Corinthians and the Corinthian column in architecture. Upstanding! The crest is the initials CFC.

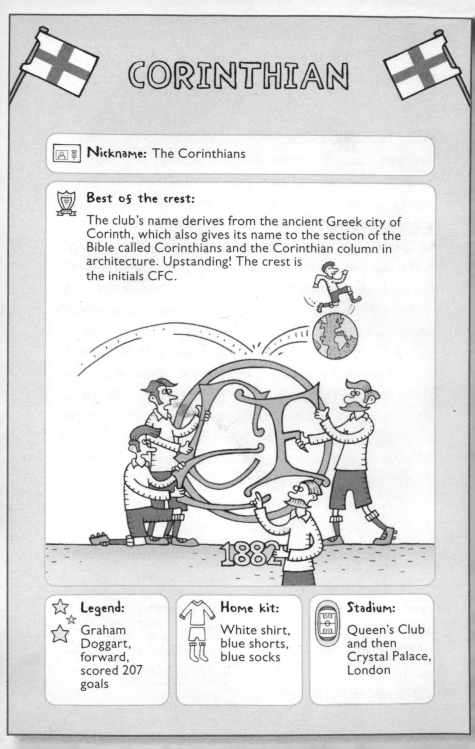

1882

Legend:
Graham Doggart, forward, scored 207 goals

Home kit:
White shirt, blue shorts, blue socks

Stadium:
Queen's Club and then Crystal Palace, London

Globetrotting amateurs who made the world love soccer

Corinthian might just be the most influential football club in the world. This amateur team played an important role in the early development of the England national team. They also helped to introduce football to the wider world in the early 1900s by touring Europe, Africa, the USA and South America. Without the Corinthians, football might not be the global game it is today!

The club was set up in 1882 by senior figures at the English FA, after the England team lost heavily to Scotland in three successive matches. The FA assistant secretary Nicholas Lane Jackson thought that having a group of players who trained together regularly would improve the national team – and he was right.

In 1888, England finally beat Scotland 5–0 – thanks to the nine Corinthian players in the team. In 1894, England beat Wales 6–0 with a team made up entirely of Corinthians. Corinthian is still the only team to provide an entire England eleven.

Some of their players also excelled in other sports: Corinthian defender CB Fry played both cricket and football for England. Over! Max Woosnam was a defender who also played tennis: he won a Wimbledon title and an Olympic gold medal. Smashing! Johnny Douglas boxed at the Olympics, while goalkeeper Benjamin Baker was an Olympic high jumper and triple jumper. These players truly hit the heights!

ROGUE IN BROGUES

Corinthian striker Tinsley Lindley scored fourteen goals in thirteen England games – wearing his normal shoes! He said football boots were too heavy and affected his speed!

Because Corinthian were an amateur club, they only played friendly matches. They might have taken the friendliness too far at times, as the team were famous for their good sportsmanship. They thought a player would never foul someone on purpose, so if a penalty was given, their goalkeeper would stand beside the post and let the opposition kicker score. When Corinthian were awarded penalties, their captain would deliberately miss the target. This attitude led to the phrase "Corinthian spirit", used to describe the highest standard of sportsmanship.

The Corinthians had a strong belief in playing just for the love of the game. They refused to turn professional and, because of their amateur status, in 1907 the FA banned the club from playing any matches against professional teams in England.

In response, the Corinthians decided to play their matches abroad. Between 1904 and 1911, they travelled to fourteen countries across the world. They made such an impression in Spain that the newly formed Real Madrid decided to wear a white kit in their honour.

They also brought the competitive game outside of Europe for the first time, travelling to South Africa (1897) and the USA (1904). One of their former players, Charles Miller, helped arrange the matches for their Brazil tour in 1910, and it was their most successful. The Corinthians were such a hit in São Paulo, the biggest city in South America, that within a few days five railway workers had founded their own team named after the English visitors. Today, Corinthians are the biggest club in São Paulo and have won more than 30 Brazilian league titles, one Copa Libertadores (the South American version of the Champions League) and two FIFA Club World Cup titles.

By the 1930s, professional football was attracting more fans than amateur football, as well as better players, so in 1939 Corinthian decided to merge with another amateur club, the Casuals FC. The new team was called the Corinthian-Casuals. They still play today, and remain true to their founding principles of amateurism and fair play.

In 1988, the Corinthian-Casuals were invited to Brazil to celebrate the one-hundredth birthday of the São Paulo Corinthians. The Brazilians beat their English namesakes 1–0, with the scorer the former Brazil midfielder Sócrates (who played much of the second half for the Corinthian-Casuals). For two teams named after a Greek city, the fact that the scorer was named after a Greek philosopher was the perfect result!

DICK, KERR LADIES

Best of the crest:

In their early days, the club did not use a crest. When they represented England against France, however, the badge was a white rose and a crown. The royal roses!

Legend:

Lily Parr, winger, scored roughly 900 goals

Home kit:

Black and white shirt, blue shorts, black and white socks

Stadium:

Deepdale, Preston, cap. 10,000

Factory team was a football machine

You've probably never heard of Dick, Kerr Ladies. Few people have these days. But a century ago they were the most terrific team in the country. They played to packed stadiums, their players were celebrities and they represented England in the first ever women's international game. Dick, Kerr were the club to beat during a brief, unexpected period in British history when women's football was as popular as men's. Fantas-Dick, Kerr-azy times!

The first thing that seems unusual about the team is their name, which has a boy's name and a comma in it. Punctuation pioneers! The confusing name, however, is due to the fact that the team were all workers at the Dick, Kerr & Co factory in Preston.

Dick, Kerr & Co made machinery for railways, and at the beginning of the twentieth century the workers were men. This all changed when, in 1914, Britain declared war on Germany. It was the beginning of what would later be known as the First World War. The Dick, Kerr factory, like many others in the UK, switched to producing military equipment and weapons. Since so many men were sent to the trenches to fight, the factory began to hire women in their place. In fact, during the war, women stepped in to do many jobs traditionally done by men, such as delivery driver, farmer and police officer.

Women also started to do other things that had previously been associated with men, like playing football. Many factories established their own women's teams. In 1917,

ON THE HEAD!

Dick, Kerr players wore exactly the same style kit as men, apart from striped bonnets they used to cover their hair.

the Dick, Kerr women's team challenged a team from another Preston factory, Arundel Coulthard Foundry, to a match to raise money for charity. It took place on Christmas Day at Deepdale, the ground of the city's professional club, Preston North End, which was lying unused since all men's football had been cancelled because of the war. It was the first ever women's match in a professional-standard stadium, and a huge crowd – more than 10,000 people – showed up.

Over the next few years, women's football grew and grew, and Dick, Kerr established themselves as the best team around. They started off using only local talent, but soon were recruiting players from further afield. In 1919, the coach invited Lily Parr, a fourteen-year-old winger who played for St Helens, near Liverpool, to move to Preston so she could join the team. Parr was a phenomenon! Six feet tall and with a thunderous kick, she scored 108 goals in her first year at the club and was quickly heralded as the best player in the country.

In 1920, Dick, Kerr confirmed their number-one status when they beat a side made up of the best players from the rest of England. That year, the team scored another first when they played a visiting team from France in the first ever international match in women's football. They also travelled to France where they were unbeaten against French teams. Attendance of women's football continued to grow, and at the end of 1920, more than 53,000 people crammed into Everton's stadium at Goodison Park to watch Dick, Kerr beat arch-rivals St Helens 4–0.

Yet the popularity of women's football did not please everyone. The Football Association, the sport's governing body, did not like the way that women's football was taking attention away from the men's game, which had restarted after the end of the war. The FA, which was run by men, also believed (wrongly!) that physical exercise was unsuitable for women. As a result, the FA banned professional clubs from hosting games for women's teams. The ban was a devastating blow to the women's game, since women's teams could no longer play to big crowds, and sadly the public soon lost interest.

Dick, Kerr carried on playing, changed their name to Preston Ladies and in 1937 were declared "Champions of the World" when they beat Scottish champions the Edinburgh Ladies. Lily Parr carried on playing until 1951, with a career total of around 900 goals.

In 1971, the FA overturned the ban on women playing in stadiums and women's football began to grow again. But no matter how successful any team ever become, the first great women's team will always be Dick, Kerr Ladies.

LILY PARR

DONCASTER BELLES

Nickname: The Belles

Best of the crest:

The Belles' crest has a Viking and a sword, which is copied from the crest of sibling club Doncaster Rovers. The white rose is a symbol of Yorkshire.

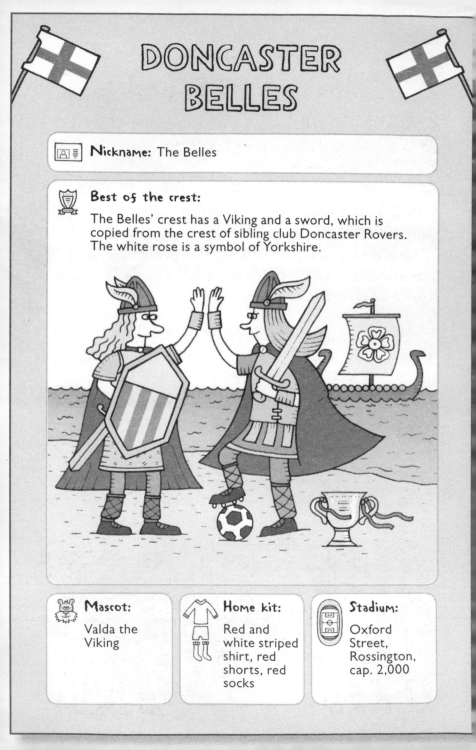

Mascot:

Valda the Viking

Home kit:

Red and white striped shirt, red shorts, red socks

Stadium:

Oxford Street, Rossington, cap. 2,000

The Yorkshire women who conquered England

Sheila Stocks and her friends formed a football club that went on to become the most terrific team in the country. The Doncaster Belles were the stars of women's football during a decade in which the sport was finally getting national recognition. In 1992, the club won the first English league without losing a single game. Unbeata-Belles!

Sheila grew up in Doncaster, South Yorkshire. In 1969, aged sixteen, she had a Saturday job selling lottery tickets at Doncaster Rovers' stadium, Belle Vue, during home games. She enjoyed watching the football so much that she started a women's team for her and her pals. They originally called themselves the Belle Vue Belles, after the stadium, but soon changed their name to the Doncaster Belles.

At that time, women's football had few spectators and little money, the result of an FA ban on women's teams playing in the stadiums of professional clubs. In 1971, however, the FA overturned the ban and women's football started to grow. The Belles were helped out by the players' mums and dads, siblings and cousins, boyfriends and girlfriends.

GO, BELLES!

Sheila's dad found out there was a women's league in nearby Sheffield, which the Belles entered in 1972. When that league closed down, the Belles joined the Nottinghamshire League in 1975, a little further south. The Belles became the outstanding team in that league. Sheila put that down to the sense of community they all felt, and the fact that the more they succeeded, the more other good players wanted to join.

Even with their success in the regional league, the Belles were still playing in parks and organising raffles to raise money for travel. But they kept on improving and, in 1983, they made it to the final of the FA Cup, the only national competition open to women, since there was no national league. The match, held at Lincoln City's Sincil Bank Stadium, was the first time the Belles played on a professional pitch. They had tracksuits made for the day, paid for by the players' proud parents, so that they would look professional as they walked on to the pitch. The Belles won the game, with striker Sheila netting two goals, one with each foot. The team were now champions of England!

Sheila's day job was as head of sport at a Doncaster secondary school. The year of her FA Cup victory, a new PE teacher arrived: Paul Edmunds, an ex-footballer who had played at Leicester City and Bournemouth. Paul became the Belles' coach, and his professional expertise helped them maintain their position as the dominant team in the country for the next decade. And another thing too: Sheila and Paul fell in love and got married! Ding-dong, wedding Belles!

The Doncaster Belles reached the FA Cup final every year except one between 1983 and 1994, winning six times. The Belles had the best players in the country. "There was a time the team had eight or nine internationals in it, which was amazing," said Sheila. One of their star players, Doncaster girl Gillian Coultard, joined when she was only thirteen. Coultard was called up by England when she was eighteen, and went on to be the first woman to play 100 times for the Lionesses.

The growth in interest in women's football convinced the FA to begin a national league. The Belles won the first competition, in 1991, winning every single game, and took the trophy again two years later. Yet as women's football became more popular, it began to change. Top professional clubs, like Arsenal and Liverpool, started to invest in women's teams, and smaller clubs like the Belles, who were not affiliated to professional clubs, were unable to afford the best players or facilities. Slowly the Belles dropped down the divisions and even though they merged with Doncaster Rovers (changing their name to Doncaster Rovers Belles and playing in the Rovers colours), they now compete in the fourth tier of English football.

The Belles may not be ringing as loudly as they were in the 1980s, but their fame and success reverberates through the women's game to this day. They remain the Belles of the ball!

BRILL GILL

In 2021, Belles midfield legend Gillian Coultard became one of only a few women footballers to receive an MBE – a top national honour – for services to football. Very Coul!

ENGLAND

Nickname: The Three Lions

Best of the crest:

Three lions have featured on the UK's royal coat of arms since the twelfth century. The ten roses represent the ten regional branches of the FA. The star represents England's 1966 World Cup victory.

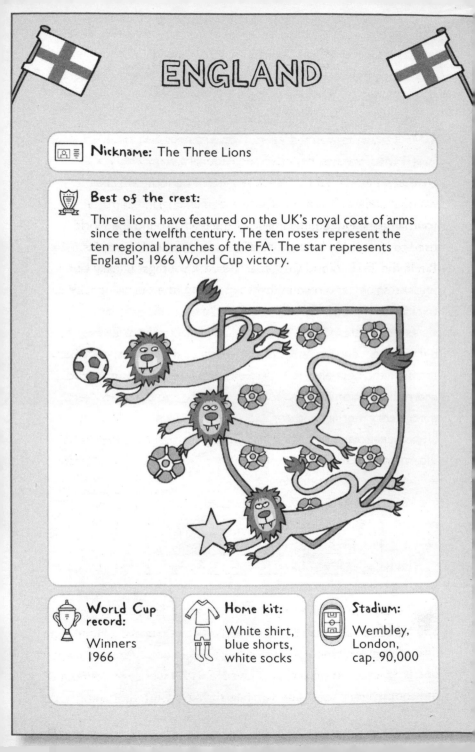

World Cup record:

Winners 1966

Home kit:

White shirt, blue shorts, white socks

Stadium:

Wembley, London, cap. 90,000

Coach inspires end
to penalty hoodoo

England have won the World Cup just once – in 1966. For many years, however, the national team were world champions at something else: losing penalty shoot-outs! No national side has lost more shoot-outs than England in major tournaments. Indeed, the image of the team around the world used to be defined by their inability to score crunch penalties. But in the 2018 World Cup, coach Gareth Southgate finally laid England's ghosts to rest. In that tournament, the team's penalty performance went from terrible to terrific!

A penalty shoot-out happens when a knockout match finishes in a draw after the extra period of 30 minutes has been played. Each team takes five penalties. Whoever scores the most wins. If the scores are *still* equal, then it's sudden death, and the teams keep going until one player scores and another misses.

Going into the 2018 World Cup, England had the tournament's worst record for penalty shoot-outs – three defeats out of three:

WORLD CUP	ROUND	OPPONENT	SCORE
1990	Semi-final	Germany	3–4
1998	Round of 16	Argentina	3–4
2006	Quarter-final	Portugal	1–3

The England coach knew all too well about England's penalty pain. Southgate had been part of the team that met Germany in the semi-final of Euro 96, which also went to penalties. Southgate had stepped up... And when his penalty was saved, England were knocked out of the competition. Southgate was heartbroken. Gutted Gareth!

The trauma of his penalty miss meant that, for 2018, Southgate had developed a completely different approach to penalties from any previous England coach. First, he told his players that penalties are a skill that can be practised and improved – so if you practise well, you will get better and increase your chances of scoring. And secondly, in perhaps the most important piece of advice, he told them not to worry if they missed. The average penalty scoring record is around 80 per cent, or four out of five. It's perfectly normal for at least one of the five players to miss a penalty. They mustn't let it shake their confidence!

England's first opponents in the knockout stage of the tournament were Colombia. When the game ended 1–1, it meant penalties would decide the winner. But this time England were ready for it. They had prepared!

Colombia scored first. 1–0. Then Harry Kane stepped up and . . . scored. 1–1. Colombia scored again. 2–1. Marcus Rashford took the next penalty and . . . scored. 2–2. Colombia scored again. 3–2. Jordan Henderson was up next and . . . his kick was saved! The score remained 3–2.

The players remembered Southgate's advice. It's fine to miss one penalty. You can still recover. Colombia took the next and . . . it was saved! Still 3–2. Kieran Trippier took England's next penalty and . . . scored! 3–3.

Colombia took their fifth penalty and . . . England saved it again! 3–3. It was now down to the fifth England penalty-taker. If he scored, England were through. Up stepped Eric Dier. He had been practising for ages. Dier took the shot and . . . scored! 3–4! England had won a World Cup penalty shoot-out at last and were through.

The whole country celebrated. England had lost five shoot-outs in a row (three in a World Cup and two in Euros), but now their penalty hoodoo was finally over. England beat Sweden in the next round but lost 2–1 to Croatia in the semi-final. The players – and Southgate – came home as heroes.

The penalty success was no fluke. England won their next shoot-out, 6–5, against Switzerland in the 2019 UEFA Nations League. Among the scorers was Jordan Pickford, the England goalkeeper, which made him the first England goalkeeper to score a penalty. Pick that one out!

England's new-found penalty success shows it is always possible to overcome your demons. There might be some tough moments along the way, as Southgate knows all too well, but you will get there in the end. Penalty, anyone? Bring it on!

 CAPTAIN KANE!

Harry Kane is the highest-scoring England captain in history. Lucky for England that he chose to play for them – he could have played for Ireland as his dad was born there!

ENGLAND WOMEN

🪪 **Nickname:** The Lionesses

🛡️ **Best of the crest:**

The lions on the crest are striding, with their right forepaws raised, positioned sideways and looking at the viewer. This is a style known by heraldry boffins as "lions passant guardant". Pass the ball and guard the goal, Lionesses!

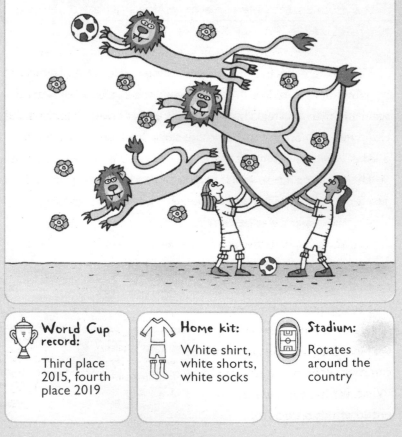

🏆 **World Cup record:**

Third place 2015, fourth place 2019

👕 **Home kit:**

White shirt, white shorts, white socks

🏟️ **Stadium:**

Rotates around the country

Big cats ready to pounce on titles

England are double World Cup semi-finalists, which means that they have twice been one of the four most terrific teams in international women's football. On both occasions, in 2015 and 2019, they were knocked out by the most terrifically tiny margin.

In the 2015 World Cup semi-final, the Lionesses were holding Japan 1–1 with only a few seconds left on the clock. At that point defender Laura Bassett, trying to cut out a cross, somehow flicked the ball from distance into her own net. It was a freakish, unlucky goal that broke the nation's hearts.

In the 2019 World Cup semi-final, England faced USA, the reigning champions. In a game full of twists and turns, USA took an early lead before Ellen White levelled the scores. USA scored again and then White scored – but it was disallowed. It looked like USA were on course for the final until England were awarded a penalty with a few minutes left to play. England now had a chance. Steph Houghton, the skipper, stepped up to take the spot kick. The country held its breath . . . but her kick lacked power and USA's goalkeeper saved it. USA held on to win 2–1.

With two super-close, nail-biting semi-finals under their belts, the Lionesses are hoping that at the next World Cup it will be third time lucky, and we have faith that the Lionesses can roar all the way to the final. Whatever happens, we are proud of this pride!

FARA-WAY IN THE LEAD

The most capped Lioness is Fara Williams, who has played for her country 172 times.

FC NORDSJÆLLAND

Nickname: *Tigrene* (The Tigers)

Best of the crest:
A tiger. Raaaaaarrr!

Mascot:
Timba the tiger

Home kit:
Red shirt, red shorts, red socks

Stadium:
Right to Dream Park, Farum, cap. 10,000

Young guns winning in a different way

Danish club FC Nordsjælland (pronounced FC Nor-shay-land, but usually known by the initials FCN) are the youngest team, based on the ages of the players, in a top European league. The club is also on a mission to educate all its players in how football can help make the world a better place. This is one football school that we definitely support!

When FCN beat AGF Aarhus 1–0 in March 2021, they made history as the youngest team ever to win a match in the Superliga, Denmark's top division. The average age of FCN players in the game was 20.8 years old – and the oldest player was only 24! That's younger than the average age of players in Denmark, which is 26.1 years old. (The Premier League average is even older: 26.9 years old.)

The youngsters' victory in 2021 was just the latest achievement of a club with a unique approach to developing their players. FCN do not measure success by trophies. They are more interested in developing future role models who care about others. The training staff believe that this type of education makes youngsters better people – and better players!

For example, the club has a coach whose job it is to help develop players' personalities. This coach works on character traits that can influence both sporting and life success.

ZEE VS ZEA

Nordsjælland means "North Zealand", because the club is based in the north of Denmark's Zealand island. The country New Zealand, however, was named after the Dutch region Zeeland. ConfuZEEng!

The traits on their curriculum are in the list below. How many do you think you have, and where could you improve?

1. Self-discipline
2. Integrity
3. Initiative
4. The drive to win
5. Giving back
6. Social intelligence
7. Passion

The club's owners also run Africa's top football youth academy, Right to Dream, which is based in Ghana. Many young Ghanaians graduate from Right to Dream and end up playing for FCN. The academy has produced more than 20 players for the Ghana national team. But the traffic is not just one way.

All the young Danish players at FCN also spend time in Africa, where they mix with their Ghanaian team-mates, in order to learn about a different culture. As a result, the squad is full of young players from different countries who enjoy friendship and mutual respect. This experience builds character as much as it creates great footballers.

FCN don't demand their players do extra running or skills sessions. Instead, each player in every age category is given a project where they have to help in the community. For example, one senior player built a mosque in his hometown, while a fourteen-year-old helped a homeless man he met at his local bus stop. That's training for life!

You might think that picking players mostly between 18 and 22 and asking them to spend lots of their time doing non-football work is not a very sensible way to build up a successful team. Wrong! FCN usually finish in the top half of the Superliga. They even won the league title in 2012, catapulting some of their players into the Denmark national team. And that young team who beat AGF Aarhus to create a Danish record? It included ELEVEN players who came through the club's academy system: six from Denmark, and five from Right to Dream. Top of the class! FCN are happy to sell their best talent every year, because there are always younger players from the academy ready to replace them.

The club's success has not gone unnoticed. In 2021, one of Egypt's biggest companies paid for a new Right to Dream academy to be built in Egypt to develop and educate the next generation of players there. Soon FCN will have more African talent in its team!

Promoting equal opportunities for boys and girls is also a huge part of the club's success. Their women's team recently won three promotions in a row to compete in the Danish first division.

We love this club where you are guaranteed a great education, learn how to be socially responsible – and play great football. We are wild about the Tigers!

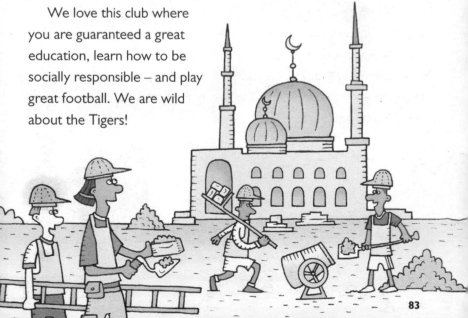

FOREST GREEN ROVERS

Best of the crest:

The crest might look like a medieval coat of arms, but the lion and the unicorn were only introduced in 2011. The lion represents power, while the unicorn gives a sense of magic.

Mascot:

The Green Devil

Home kit:

Black and green shirts, green shorts, black and green socks

Stadium:

The New Lawn, Nailsworth, cap. 5,000

The team who are saving the planet, one vegan burger at a time!

Forest Green Rovers are a tree-fic team! They have twigged on to the fact that we need to protect the environment, and are doing amazing things to achieve that goal. They believe they can change football and the world! We're rooting for them!

Based in Nailsworth, Gloucestershire, Forest Green were promoted to League Two in 2017 and are shooting upwards! Yet what has got them noticed around the world is not their football, but rather the environmentally friendly projects they have put in place. At Forest Green:

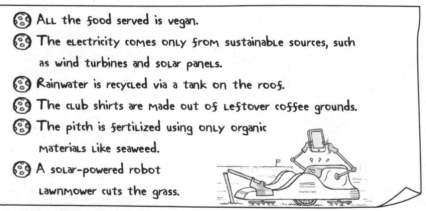

- All the food served is vegan.
- The electricity comes only from sustainable sources, such as wind turbines and solar panels.
- Rainwater is recycled via a tank on the roof.
- The club shirts are made out of leftover coffee grounds.
- The pitch is fertilized using only organic materials like seaweed.
- A solar-powered robot lawnmower cuts the grass.

The club's approach to sustainability and recycling has won international acclaim. FIFA named Forest Green the greenest club in the world. The United Nations went even further and have awarded Forest Green a special certificate for being the greenest professional sports organisation in the world. (Here "green" means concerned with protecting the environment, although the club also scores high on other measures of greenness – their kit is lime green and black, and they have green in their name.)

Forest Green can boast another record too. Nailsworth is the smallest town ever to host a team in the Football League, meaning one of the top four tiers. The town has a population of about 6,000 people – not many more than a village. In fact, for about 100 years, Forest Green only played in regional, semi-professional leagues. All that changed in 2010, when a maverick local businessman called Dale Vince took over the club. Not only did Vince put money into the club for buying players and improving facilities, but he decided to make the club as environmentally sustainable as possible. "We've got to change the way we live," said Vince, "and here at Forest Green we're always finding things in football that can be changed."

Thanks to Vince's innovations, Forest Green are leading the way in showing how football  can help tackle climate change. One of the human activities that contributes most to climate change is the burning of fossil fuels, such as coal, to make electricity.  Vince owns a company that generates electricity from wind and solar power, and his company supplies all of Forest Green's electricity.

Vince is also a vegan, which means that he eats no animal products, including meat, milk and eggs. He made the club vegan too – which means no beef burgers on sale at half-time and no cow's milk in your tea! Vince's main reason for turning the club vegan is the environmental impact of farming livestock and the welfare of the animals. However, many sportspeople – including footballers – swear that being a vegan is healthier and improves their performance on the pitch.

In 2017, Forest Green were promoted to League Two for the first time in their history. They quickly showed themselves to be one of the strongest teams in the league. Vince's aim is for the club to reach the Championship and, in preparation for bigger crowds, he is replacing the club's 2,000-seater stadium with a brand-new stadium which will seat 5,000, and will be the largest football stadium in the world to be built almost entirely from wood. Wood is better for the environment than materials such as steel and concrete, which are normally used to build stadiums.

The club has also been innovative in clothing design, trying to eliminate the plastic contained in most sportswear. Forest Green are the first team to wear kit made from recycled coffee grounds. Vince says the shirts are more breathable – and they don't smell of coffee!

Forest Green's mission to be as green as can be has won them fans around the world. One international footballer, the Spanish defender Héctor Bellerín, liked what they were doing so much he has invested his own money in the club. "People have a universal love of football, so there is no better industry to promote sustainability," he said.

Forest Green's football seedlings are sprouting upwards! Here's to a future forest of vic-trees for this super green eco-team!

A DAZZLE OF ZEBRAS

Dale Vince changed Rovers' kit to zebra stripes after learning that the zebra's striped pattern confuses predators by making it harder to judge speed and direction. Vince will be hoping the same thing happens to the team's opponents!

FRANCE

Nickname: *Les Bleus* (The Blues)

Best of the crest:

The cockerel is a symbol of France, thanks to some ancient wordplay. The Latin word *gallus*, meaning "cockerel", and *Gallus*, meaning "Gaul", the ancient region that roughly corresponds to where France is now, are spelt the same.

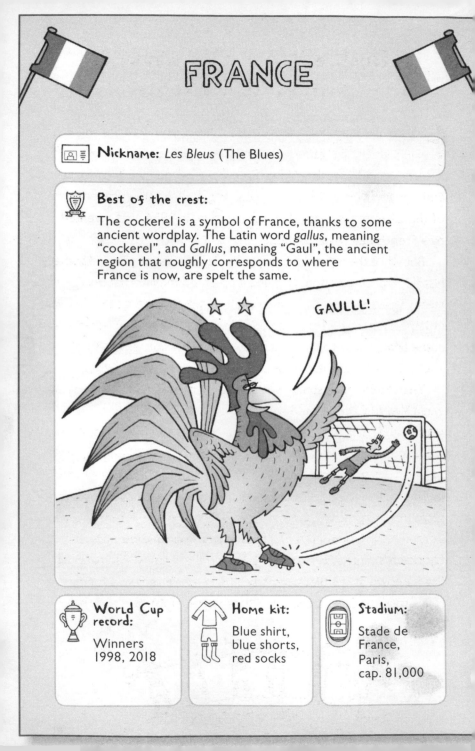

GAULLL!

World Cup record:
Winners 1998, 2018

Home kit:
Blue shirt, blue shorts, red socks

Stadium:
Stade de France, Paris, cap. 81,000

Double World Cup winners with worldwide roots

France invented international football. *Oui*, you read that right! FIFA, the global game's governing body, was set up and led by a Frenchman in 1904; the World Cup was invented by a Frenchman and was first held in 1930; and the European Cup (the predecessor of the Champions League), which launched in 1954, was invented by a Frenchman. *Vive La France!*

But while these French innovators played a major part in football history, France traditionally found it tough on the international stage. That all changed when the country hosted its first World Cup in 1998. France lifted the trophy for the first time, beating Brazil 3–0 in the final, thanks to two goals from Zinedine Zidane, a magical midfielder, who at the time was voted the world's best player.

The 1998 France squad were the most diverse team ever to win a World Cup, a proud showcase of multicultural France. The players had roots in every continent as well as Europe: Africa (Zidane's parents came from Algeria; defender Marcel Desailly was born in Ghana), North America (defender Lilian Thuram was born in the Caribbean), South America (striker David Trezeguet's parents were from Argentina), Oceania (midfielder Christian Karembeu was born in New Caledonia in the Pacific) and Asia (midfielder Youri Djorkaeff's mum was Armenian). In fact, the team whose national flag is known as the *Bleu-blanc-rouge* (Blue-white-red) was fondly nicknamed the *Black-blanc-beur* (Black-white-Arab).

France is home to millions of immigrants – that is, people who were born in other countries but moved to live there – and millions of children of these immigrants. Many have roots in African countries, like Algeria and Senegal, that France used to rule over. The 1998 victory gave the French a sense of pride about their multicultural country.

Yet the promise of racial harmony was short-lived, replaced by rising tensions and violence. In 2005, many young people, mostly of African and Arab heritage, rioted across France in protest at the lack of jobs and unfair treatment by the police.

Around the same time, the national team were facing their own problems. France's players were often caught behaving unprofessionally, the coach made racist comments and, at the 2010 World Cup, the team went on strike and refused to train.

It took Didier Deschamps, captain of the 1998 World-Cup-winning side, to turn the national team around. When he was appointed coach, he gave the players strict rules of behaviour they had to follow if they wanted to play for France. If anyone misbehaved, they were out! His team slowly won over the fans and narrowly lost the 2016 Euros final to Portugal. They vowed to do better at the 2018 World Cup.

They did just that, thanks to one player who embodies the best of modern-day France's diversity: Kylian Mbappé is the son of a Cameroonian father and an Algerian mother and grew up in the Paris suburbs.

Mbappé was *magnifique* at the 2018 World Cup, scoring two goals and setting up another in a stunning 4–3 win over Lionel Messi's Argentina. He then scored in France's 4–2 win over Croatia in the final – becoming the first teenager to score in the final since Pelé back in 1958. By the time he was 21, Mbappé had already won the French league title with Monaco and three league titles with Paris Saint-Germain – not to mention the World Cup!

Mbappé is the perfect role model for France today. His heritage is African, he plays with intelligence and speed, and as a person he is honest and generous. He donated his World Cup winner's bonus payment to charity and has set up his own foundation to help children in Paris. His talent enabled France to reach the top of world football again, and his actions and words, on and off the pitch, helped to bring together a divided nation.

We owe great thanks to France for inventing international football and setting up exciting competitions like the World Cup and the Champions League. Imagine how dull life would be without them. And in winning the 1998 World Cup with such an international team, France also reminded us that we are all stronger together. *Allez les Bleus!*

FOUR, TWO!

The most frequent result in a World Cup final is 4–2, which has now happened four times, including when France won in 2018 and when England won in 1966.

GERMANY

Nickname: *Die Mannschaft* (The Team)

Best of the crest:

The black eagle is taken from Germany's coat of arms. It has been a symbol of the German people for almost a thousand years, making it the oldest national symbol in Europe.

World Cup record:

Winners 1954, 1974, 1990 and 2014

Home kit:

White shirt, black shorts, white socks

Stadium:

Rotates around the country

The reign that started in the rain

It's hard to believe, but there used to be a time when Germany were the underdogs. Nowadays, Germany are always near the top of the world rankings. The country has a reputation for physically and psychologically strong players, who have made the Mannschaft arguably the most consistent team in international football. Between 1954 and 2014, Germany qualified for every single World Cup and never placed lower than the quarter-finals, winning the tournament four times. *Sehr gut, ja!*

At the start of the 1954 World Cup, however, Germany were just another team, considered neither the best in the world nor even the best in Europe. (Back then, the team was called West Germany, since at that time the country was split into two parts, East and West.) In the group stage, Hungary, who had not lost a match for four years, humiliated the Germans by winning 8–3. When the two teams met again for the final, Hungary were the sure favourites to win. Yet the match became one of the most dramatic, intriguing and controversial finals in World Cup history – and it was all because of the weather.

On the day of the final, in Bern, Switzerland, West Germany coach Sepp Herberger looked out of the window of his hotel room. A sunny morning had given way to rain. "It's Fritz Walter weather," he declared with a smile. Walter was the team's star striker, who always played better in wet conditions. Herberger knew he needed all the help he could get against the in-form Hungarians.

The game started predictably: after eight minutes, Hungary were 2–0 ahead. It looked like West Germany were heading for an even heavier defeat than in the group stage. But the team, inspired by Walter, clawed it back. They scored twice before the break, with Walter setting up both goals. The half-time score was 2–2. By now, both sets of players were slipping in the wet conditions.

Herberger had a trick up his sleeve for the break. He had asked his friend, German shoemaker Adi Dassler, to create boots for his team to wear. Dassler provided the team with the first ever boots to have screw-in studs, which meant you could change the type of stud if the weather conditions changed. At half-time, Herberger turned to Dassler and said: "Adi, studs on!" Dassler, who had sat on the West Germany bench during the match and was allowed inside the dressing room, told the players to switch studs and put in the longer ones. The longer studs would help them keep their balance on the wet and slippery pitch.

It worked a treat! The West Germany players coped much better in the torrential conditions than Hungary, even though the favourites kept on creating chances. West Germany goalkeeper Toni Turek saved almost everything that came his way – and when he didn't, a defender was there to make a goal-line clearance.

With just over five minutes left, Helmut Rahn scored for West Germany to complete an improbable comeback. No one could believe it! Even the commentator reporting on the game exclaimed: "Germany lead 3–2! Call me mad, call me crazy!" West Germany held on to win – but only after the referee controversially disallowed a Hungary goal for being offside. The match became known as the Miracle of Bern, and is considered one of the greatest World Cup shocks.

The victory gave confidence and pride to a generation of Germans who had lived through the Second World War, which had begun in 1939 and ended in 1945. Germany had lost the war and Germans were ashamed of how their country had behaved. The Miracle of Bern also marked the introduction of a new football powerhouse to world

SERGING AHEAD

Striker Serge Gnabry, who started his career at Arsenal, scored a hat-trick on his Germany debut in 2018. It was against San Marino and Germany won 8–0.

football: one with a never-give-up attitude that continues to this day. In 1990, East and West Germany united and the two teams began to play as a single Germany team. (The first match of the united Germany team took place a few months after West Germany won the 1990 World Cup.) Germany won the World Cup for the first time as a united team in 2014.

And what about shoemaker Dassler? He went on to set up a business which he named after the first syllables of his name: Adidas, now one of the biggest sports brands in the world!

BROTHERS AT WAR

Adi Dassler had a brother, Rudi, who was also a shoemaker. (They both learned shoemaking from their dad.) Adi and Rudi started by working together, but after a bitter falling-out, Rudi left and set up his own shoe company, Puma, in the same village as Adi's company, Adidas. Their rivalry spurred each other on!

IRAQ

Nickname: The Lions of Mesopotamia

Best of the crest:

The Arabic words on the crest say *Allahu Akbar*, meaning "God is the greatest", a common Muslim expression. The white star represents the 2007 Asian Cup victory.

World Cup record:

One appearance, 1986

Home kit:

White shirt, white shorts, white socks

Stadium:

Basra International, Basra, cap. 65,000

Fairytale victory brings happiness to a nation at war

Iraq's triumph at the 2007 Asian Cup was one of the most unexpected victories in international football. Not only were Iraq, on paper, one of the weakest teams in the tournament, but the country was in the middle of a bloody war in which different Iraqi groups were fighting each other. Iraq's terrific title united the country in joy, showing how football can bring enemies together.

The Asian Cup is the Asian equivalent of the Euros. Iraq qualified for the 2007 event after playing its home games in the nearby United Arab Emirates. (Playing in Iraq was too dangerous because of the fighting.) A few months before the Cup was due to begin, the Iraq FA hired Brazilian Jorvan Vieira as coach. Vieira had never coached at that level before and was the fourth choice for the job. It was hardly a dream start to the campaign!

Vieira got his team together in neighbouring Jordan, where they could train in relative safety. Quite apart from the usual challenges of getting the squad fit and practising set pieces, he also had to cope with the players' mental states. Everyone knew someone who had been affected by the violence in Iraq. The goalkeeper, for example, had seen a family member killed. "It was the hardest job in the world," said Vieira. "I was trainer, psychologist, father, brother, friend. I wanted to be everything to these players, to help them use football as a way to escape these terrible things happening to their country."

WHERE IT ALL BEGAN

Iraq is situated on land known in ancient times as Mesopotamia, which was home to the world's earliest civilisation. It was here that numbers and writing were invented.

At the beginning of the tournament, no one gave Iraq a chance. The favourites were South Korea, Japan, Saudi Arabia and Australia. Iraq drew their first game 1–1 against fellow minnows Thailand. But it was only in their second game, a shock 3–1 victory over an Australia team boasting Premier League players, that Iraq began to believe a miracle was possible. Iraq qualified top of their group and then dispatched Vietnam in the quarter-finals. In the semi-finals, they edged South Korea on penalties.

By now, Iraqis back home were ecstatic about how unexpectedly well the team were performing. Yet this happiness would soon turn to horror. Thirty fans celebrating the semi-final victory in the streets of Baghdad, the Iraq capital, were killed when a bomb exploded in an ice-cream parlour.

The nation was in mourning. The players briefly considered abandoning the tournament as a mark of respect. But as they watched the news, they saw a bereaved woman, hysterical after the death of her son, begging the team to continue in his memory. That made up their minds: they would play in the final against Saudi Arabia and do their best to bring happiness to a country desperately in need of it. The Iraq players came from the different parts of the country that were fighting against each other. The tragedy made them more determined than ever to put their beliefs aside for the sake of football and peace.

Since no one had expected Iraq to reach the final, the team had not even booked a pitch to train on. They practised for the match in a local park, watched by bemused onlookers. On the way to the final, in Jakarta, Indonesia, coach Vieira had a nap on the team bus. In a bid to conquer his players' nerves, he wanted to show them how relaxed he was!

On the pitch, Iraq held off the Saudi threat for the first half and, fifteen minutes from time, captain Younis Mahmoud jumped highest to head in a free kick. Striker Mahmoud, nicknamed Desert Fox for his ability to find himself in the right place at the right time, was always the most likely to score a match-winner. Iraq held on to win 1– 0. The country was able to celebrate its first ever Asian Cup victory.

Against a background of bloodshed, the Iraq team were a beacon of national unity and pride. They showed how people with different beliefs can work together and succeed. "It doesn't matter what I am," said Mahmoud. "Above all else, I am Iraqi."

ITALY

Best of the crest:

The Italian flag is set in a shield. The four stars represent each of Italy's World Cup triumphs.

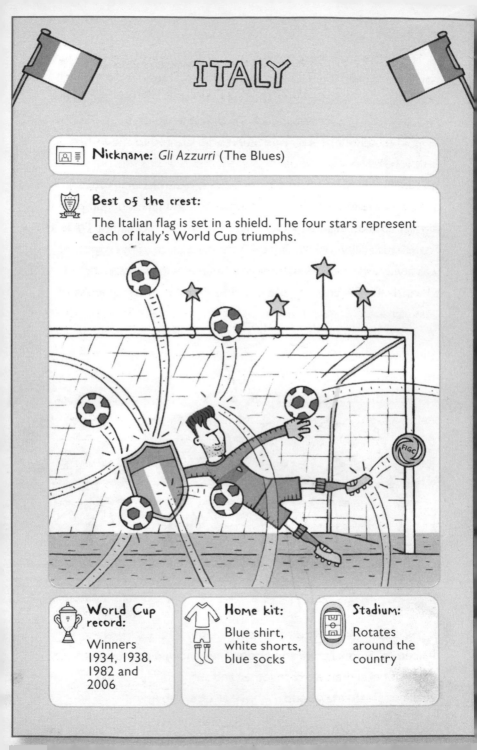

World Cup record:

Winners 1934, 1938, 1982 and 2006

Home kit:

Blue shirt, white shorts, blue socks

Stadium:

Rotates around the country

The top team whose brightest stars are always in defence

The country of Italy is famous for its glamour, fashion and style. So it is one of the biggest contradictions in international football that the national team plays such unfashionable football. Italy is home to Ferraris, fashion designers and fine art. Yet when it comes to football, it's the country of tough defending, few goals and stalemates. *Mamma mia*, what is going on?

The Italy team love defending. They may not always play defensively, but they have been better at defending than anyone else. Their defenders anticipate, dribble and pass more successfully than anyone, and they don't mind making tactical fouls if they see the need. One influential Italian writer said that the perfect football match would finish 0–0. That's how much they love it!

To understand the secret of Italy's defending, we need a quick Italian lesson. In Italian *catenaccio* means "door-bolt" and *libero* means "the free one". *Catenaccio* is a tactical system, mastered by Italian teams, that puts defence first by adding a *libero* behind the defenders. If the strikers get past the first line of defenders, this spare defender is waiting, marking the space. All Italian teams used to play with this system and it brought them great success.

For Italy, *catenaccio* is also a state of mind. It's a mentality that has at its heart the idea: "We must not concede a goal". And those six words have helped Italy win four World Cups – usually with the best defence and goalkeepers in the world.

ON THE SPOT

Italy were the first team to lose a World Cup final on penalties, which they did in 1994, losing to Brazil. But they were also the first team to win one on penalties, beating France in 2006.

Many young Italian footballers grow up not wanting to be creative midfielders, speedy wingers or prolific strikers. There is a feeling that a successful team can only contain one "flair" player, and these players tend to be the subject of heated public debate before big matches. Instead, Italians want to be stylish defenders or goalkeepers, because they want to follow Italy's rich tradition of heroic goal-stoppers.

That tradition began in the first World Cup Italy entered, in 1934. Italy won the tournament (of course, they conceded the fewest goals) and goalkeeper Gianpiero Combi was team captain. They won the World Cup again four years later.

Their next World Cup triumph came in 1982. Once again, they had a goalkeeper as captain (this is rare: only four goalkeepers have ever lifted the World Cup and two were Italians). Dino Zoff was the best goalkeeper in the world, and still holds the record for the most consecutive international matches without conceding a goal: twelve. Not bad for a player who was once rejected by Juventus for being too short. When he took his grandma's advice to eat eight eggs a day, he shot up, eventually signed for Juventus and won six league titles with them. Still, we don't recommend Dino's eggy diet!

By the time they won their fourth World Cup, in 2006, Italy not only had the best goalkeeper in the world, Gigi Buffon, but also the best defender, Fabio Cannavaro, who was their captain. After lifting the World Cup trophy, Cannavaro was also awarded the Ballon D'Or for the world's best player. He was the last Italian to win the coveted prize and is only the third defender in history to win it!

Even today, Italy's best players are their defenders: Giorgio Chiellini and Leonardo Bonucci are formidable centre-backs, while goalkeeper Gigi Donnarumma is set to follow in the footsteps of Combi, Zoff and Buffon. Protecting the goal at all costs!

THAT'S AMORE!

When Gigi Buffon broke the record for consecutive Serie A minutes without conceding, he wrote a love letter to his goal:

"I was 12 when I turned my back on you, denying my past to guarantee you a safe future. I went with my heart. I went with my instinct. But the day I stopped looking you in the face is also the day that I started to love you. To protect you. To be your first and last line of defence . . . We have always been opposites yet we are complementary, like the sun and the moon. Forced to live side by side without being able to touch. Team-mates for life, a life in which we are denied all contact . . . I've always thought about your welfare, putting it first even ahead of my own. I was 12 when I turned my back on my goal. And I will keep doing it as long as my legs, my head and my heart will allow."

JAPAN WOMEN

Best of the crest:

The three-legged crow is a *yatagarasu*, a creature from Japanese mythology that is seen as a symbol of divine guidance.

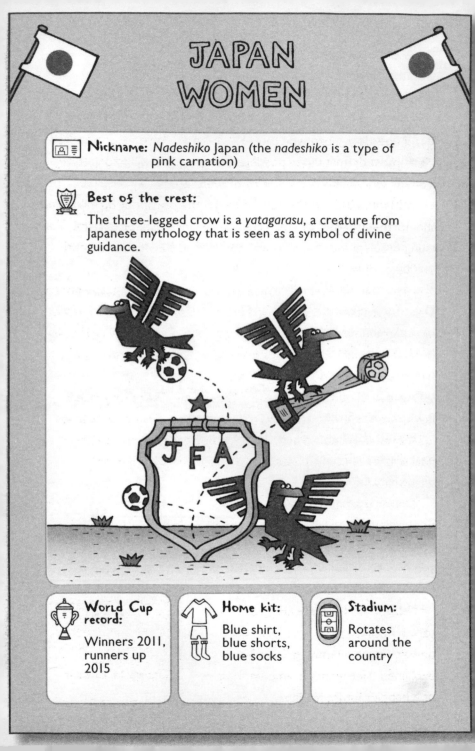

World Cup record:

Winners 2011, runners up 2015

Home kit:

Blue shirt, blue shorts, blue socks

Stadium:

Rotates around the country

World Cup winners who helped a nation in mourning

Underdogs Japan won the 2011 Women's World Cup in the most dramatic way possible, bringing joy to a nation reeling from its worst natural disaster of modern times.

In March 2011, an earthquake below the sea about 80 miles from the north-east coast of Japan created a giant wave, or tsunami. The tsunami swept into the mainland and caused the deaths of nearly 20,000 people.

Japan was still in shock when, in June, the national team went to Germany to play in the Women's World Cup. Before every game, Japan coach Norio Sasaki motivated his players by showing footage of the aftermath of the tsunami. He wanted his players to bring happiness to a nation in mourning.

Against all odds, Japan made it to the final. There they faced favourites USA, who they had not beaten in their last 25 matches. USA twice went ahead, and twice Japan equalized. The second goal was a nail-biter, scored only three minutes before the final whistle!

During the penalty shoot-out, the first three USA players all missed their penalties. Unbelievable! Japan won the shoot-out 3–1 and lifted the World Cup for the first time.

"Maybe we felt we were going to win because Japan was giving us power," captain Homare Sawa later explained. Her team became symbols of a happier future for Japan.

SUPER SAWA

Homare Sawa won the 2011 Golden Boot for top World Cup scorer. She is Japan's most capped player, with 205 appearances, and all-time top scorer with 83 goals.

JUVENTUS

Nickname: *La Vecchia Signora* (The Old Lady)

Best of the crest:

Juventus invented the practice of adding a gold star to a football shirt to denote an important title when, in 1958, they added a star to commemorate their tenth Italian league title. They now have more than 30 league titles, which gives them three stars.

Mascot:

Jay the zebra

Home kit:

Black and white striped shirt, white shorts, white socks

Stadium:

Allianz, Turin, cap. 41,000

Italy's biggest club desperate for European success

Italian titans Juventus are both Europe's most successful AND least successful elite club. They have won their national league, Serie A, more times than any other team in Europe's big four (Italy, Spain, Germany and England) have won their respective leagues. Yet Juventus are serial European also-rans, having lost the Champions League final seven times – also more times than anyone else! Winners at home, losers in Europe, the black-and-white-striped Old Lady are definitely a team of two halves!

Juventus are from Turin, the fourth biggest city in Italy, situated in the north and close to the border with France. They are by far the most popular team in the country, accounting for about one in three of all Italian football fans. The club's country-wide fan base dates back almost 100 years, and is the result of the automobile. Beep, beep!

Ever since 1923, Juventus have been owned by the Agnelli family, who also own Fiat, the largest car manufacturer in Italy, which is based in Turin. Thanks to the Agnellis' money, Juve became one of the first clubs in Italy to turn professional, and between 1931 and 1935 they won five league titles in a row. You could even say that the club won the 1934 World Cup, since for the tournament final the Italy national team included five Juventus players.

 KIDS' JOKE

The club's nickname, the Old Lady, is a joke based on the word *Juventus*, which means "youth" in Latin, the language that was spoken in Italy during the time of the Roman Empire.

You don't look old.

In fact, the wealth of the Agnelli family has meant that the club have been able to buy the best Italian players, with Juve also providing crucial members of Italy's World-Cup-winning sides in both 1982 and 2006. These include Paolo Rossi, who won the Golden Boot in 1982, and Fabio Cannavaro, who was the 2006 FIFA World Player of the Year.

Juventus's fans come from all over Italy, especially small towns and from the south of the country. There are fewer big clubs in the south, and it is less wealthy than the north, so lots of people move to Turin to make money working for Fiat. Just as the Agnellis promoted the idea that Fiat was the car for all Italians, they also presented

Juventus as the national club. And so that's what they became!

Yet Juve's power within Italian football has a dark side. In 2006, the club were relegated from Serie A for the first time because of a scandal. Juventus bosses were found to have been putting pressure on the Italian league to choose softer referees for Juventus games. Never before or since has such a big or rich club, in a top European league, faced the humiliation of forced relegation. Fans and players felt betrayed, but the team quickly recovered, returning to Serie A after only one season in Serie B.

As of early 2021, Juventus's tally of Scudettos – the badge awarded to the winners of Serie A – stood at 36, including every year since 2012, its longest ever run of back-to-back titles. You would have thought this would be more than enough to keep supporters happy. Well, *si* and *no*.

Even if they triumph at home, Juventus are eternal European underachievers. They have won the Champions League only twice: once in 1985, when it was the European Cup, and once in 1996. Compare this to the records of their Italian rivals AC Milan, who have won it seven times, and Internazionale, who have won it three times. Juve have been losing finalists seven times.

In 2017, Juventus faced Real Madrid in the Champions League final. The Italians were hammered 4–1, with Cristiano Ronaldo scoring two goals for Madrid and winning the prize for man of the match. (Ronaldo also won the Ballon D'Or that year, for the world's best player.) So what did Juventus do? They bought him!

In 2018, Juventus paid around €100 million for Ronaldo, the highest amount ever paid for a player over 30 (he was 33), and the highest amount ever paid for anyone by an Italian club. It was a high-stakes gamble for a footballer past his prime. Yet even though he has helped Juventus win two Scudettos since then, European glory remains elusive. In 2019, they only reached the quarter-finals, and in 2020 and 2021 they were knocked out in the last sixteen.

The Old Lady are desperate for another Champions League victory – and hope to see one before Ronaldo becomes an Old Man!

LEWES

Best of the crest:

The turret represents Lewes Castle and the two rooks represent the birds most often found in the stadium.

Legend:

Kelly Newton, former women's team captain

Home kit:

Red and black striped shirt, black shorts, black socks

Stadium:

The Dripping Pan, Lewes, cap. 3,000

Fan-owned club fighting for gender equality

Lewes FC is a truly global club. The Sussex side, whose women's team play in England's second tier and whose men's team play in the seventh tier, have more than 1,500 owners who live in 37 countries. This terrific team has terrific fans all over the world!

The strange set-up is a result of a group of six fans buying the club in 2010 to save it from bankruptcy. They introduced an innovative ownership system by which anyone, anywhere, could buy a tiny share of the club. More than 1,500 people did. Anyone with a share is allowed to have a say in club decisions.

The club has voted on ground-breaking policies. For example, in 2017, Lewes became the first club in the world to pay male and female athletes exactly the same wages, offer them the same resources and have them play their matches in the same stadium. They remain the only club with total equality between the men and women players, and it has brought them international recognition.

The women's team is now just one promotion away from a place in the Women's Super League, where they would rub shoulders with the likes of Arsenal, Chelsea and the Manchester clubs.

Everyone in the community is proud of Lewes and the different path they have taken. We love their approach too. When the fans have the power to decide, fairness wins and real changes happen. Fan-tastic!

ON FIRE!

Lewes is famous for its annual Bonfire Night celebrations, which are the biggest in the UK. Giant models of famous people are paraded through the town and set alight.

LIVERPOOL

🛡 **Best of the crest:**

The bird is a liver bird, a mythical creature that looks like a cormorant and is the symbol of the city of Liverpool.

LFC

Mascot:

Mighty Red the Liver Bird

Home kit:

Red shirt, red shorts, red socks

Stadium:

Anfield, Liverpool, cap. 53,000

Boot room kicks off global success

Liverpool's journey to become England's most successful football team began in a tiny, cramped and windowless room underneath the main stand at their Anfield stadium. No, we don't mean the toilet! We mean the boot room, the storeroom where the players' boots were kept between matches. It was here that coach Bill Shankly and his staff plotted to turn the Reds from also-rans into champions of England and Europe.

Shankly took over Liverpool in 1959, when the club was languishing in the Second Division. Down-to-earth and plain-speaking, the Scot was a natural leader who valued loyalty and hard work. He assembled a close-knit circle of advisers and he preferred to hold discussions with them in the boot room, sitting on upturned beer crates, rather than in comfortable chairs in his office. They discussed tactics, strategy and signings, and Liverpool's fortunes began to improve.

Shankly's high standards and attention to detail soon got the team winning. He updated the training facilities and improved the players' passing, control and concentration. The players responded well to Shankly's demands: he asked them to train as hard as they played, and established a culture of professionalism and dedication that would remain at Liverpool for decades. The team became a reflection of his own personality: hard-working, tough, persistent and creative. Promotion followed and Liverpool won the First Division in 1964.

Shankly was a master of motivation too. He understood the personality of each player and knew exactly how to get the best out of them, as individuals and as a team. In 1965, Shankly guided Liverpool to their first FA Cup final. Liverpool used to wear white shorts and striped socks, but in that game Shankly made the team

wear their now-famous all-red kit for the first time, as he thought it made the players look stronger. Liverpool beat Leeds 2–1 in the FA Cup final and the all-red kit stayed. He also put a sign above the players' tunnel that read "THIS IS ANFIELD" to intimidate the opposition. The sign is still there today.

As well as turning the team around, Shankly transformed the club's relationship with Liverpool itself. Shankly was a brilliant public speaker and made the city fall in love with the team, fostering a special relationship built around the community.

Shankly won three league titles and retired after winning the 1974 FA Cup. His replacement was Bob Paisley, who had been part of Shankly's boot-room team from the beginning.

Paisley built on Shankly's foundations and took the team to a higher level: winning six league titles and the European Cup (the predecessor of the Champions League) three times. When Paisley retired in 1983, another boot-room veteran, Joe Fagan, took over, and he won the league, the League Cup and the European Cup treble in his first year. These boot-room boys kicked it out of the park!

KOP MUSIC

In 1963, Liverpudlians Gerry and the Pacemakers released the song "You'll Never Walk Alone", from the musical *Carousel*. It caught on with Liverpool fans and became the club anthem.

When Anfield was rebuilt in the 1990s, the original boot room was knocked down and the space turned into a room for the media. In the new stadium, Liverpool failed to win a trophy for almost 20 years.

In 2015, Jürgen Klopp was appointed coach, and he led Liverpool to new success: the 2019 Champions League and the 2020 Premier League title. Like Shankly, Klopp leaned on a close circle of advisers, and, again like Shankly, Klopp was a charismatic figure able to unite the team and connect with Liverpudlians. Klopp's full-backs Trent Alexander-Arnold (12 assists) and Andy Robertson (11 assists) were attacking and creative, while his wingers, Sadio Mané (18 goals) and Mo Salah (19 goals), did not stop scoring!

Anfield's famous boot room may not exist any more, but Shankly's culture of success built on hard work, loyalty and honesty lives on. We love the Liverpool way!

LYON WOMEN

🪪 **Nickname:** *Les Fenottes* (The Women)

🛡️ **Best of the crest:**

The lion standing on one leg with its paws in the air is taken from the coat of arms of the city of Lyon. The city was the capital of Gaul, the ancient region that roughly corresponds to where France is now.

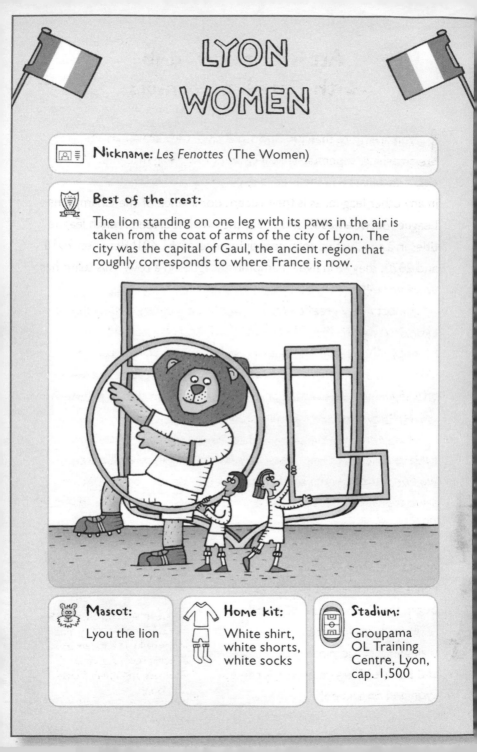

🐭 **Mascot:**

Lyou the lion

👕 **Home kit:**

White shirt, white shorts, white socks

🏟️ **Stadium:**

Groupama OL Training Centre, Lyon, cap. 1,500

All-star French club with record title hauls

Lyon are more than just a football club: they are a barrier-smashing, superstar-studded, trophy-winning machine! The club's dominance in the French league is unrivalled by any other club in any other league, as is their recent dominance of the Champions League. Between 2007 and 2020, they won fourteen French league titles in a row, with a total goal difference of +1,401! Between 2016 and 2020, they won five Champions Leagues in a row. This team has va-va-voom!

Almost every great player of the last decade has passed through Lyon, from USA's Megan Rapinoe and England's Lucy Bronze, to Norway's Ada Hegerberg and Germany's Dzsenifer Marozsán. When you put so many world-class footballers together, they challenge each other to become even better. The club is like an elite university for the sport's brightest stars.

Lyon, whose full name is Olympique Lyonnais Féminin, have achieved their successes because of a simple rule: the club treat the women's and the men's teams exactly the same. They share the same training facilities and use the same vehicles to travel to matches. (The women, however, play in a smaller stadium because their crowds are smaller.) Lyon's approach meant that from the beginning they could attract the best players, and so began the club's culture of excellence.

How much longer can the team maintain their dominance of France and Europe? They're hoping it can go Lyon and on and on!

WON FORTY-ONE

Between April 2012 and May 2013, Lyon won 41 games in a row in all competitions, a world record in both women's and men's football. *Ooh la la!*

MAKANA FOOTBALL ASSOCIATION

Best of the crest:

The Makana FA had no crest, so this image is inspired by the coat of arms of South Africa. The bird on top is the secretary bird, an African bird of prey that has an eagle-like upper body and long, thin legs.

Teams in League:

9

Years in operation:

1967–91

Venue:

Robben Island prison, South Africa

The prisoner players that built a nation

Football has the power to change lives, and in some cases even to change the destiny of a country. The teams that played in the Makana Football Association did both of these things. Here we pay tribute to nine terrific teams that triumphed in terrible times.

The Makana FA was the footballing authority in Robben Island prison, a maximum-security jail on Robben Island in South Africa. The prison, which operated between 1961 and 1991, was notorious for its brutality. Prisoners on the island did hard physical work for ten hours every day, often in the blazing sun. They were beaten regularly by the guards, slept up to 40 in a cell and were fed a diet of porridge laced with worms and bird poo.

What had these prisoners done to deserve such a horrible fate? The inmates were locked up for the supposed "crime" of speaking out against their country's racist laws, which harmed the country's Black people. In South Africa, nine out of every ten people are Black. Yet ever since the seventeenth century, when white people arrived from Europe, the white settlers had run the country and denied Black people their basic human rights. In the twentieth century, strict laws forced Black people to live, work and shop in separate, much poorer areas than white people. When the Black population began to rise up against the way they were being treated, many activists were jailed in Robben Island. The shocking, cruel behaviour of white people against Black people in South Africa was condemned all over the world.

When Robben Island prison took in its first prisoners, all recreation was banned. After three years, however, the inmates were given a football. Playing football gave the prisoners dignity and hope. "Football saved many of us," said former prisoner Lizo Sitoto. "When you were outside playing, you felt free."

The prison authorities expected the inmates to be too tired to play after all the hard labour, but the opposite happened. They invested lots of energy in the game, forming nine teams. They rolled and watered the pitch to keep it flat for the Saturday matches. They made goals out of driftwood, and nets out of fishing-nets that had washed up on the island.

The prisoners founded the Makana Football Association to run the prison league. (Makana was a Black warrior who was imprisoned on Robben Island in the eighteenth century.) Makana's officials ran it as professionally as possible. Every result – and red and yellow card – was recorded, from the first match in December 1969 until the prison closed in 1991. Friendships were made that would last for decades.

By the early 1990s, the racist South African government had agreed to give up its power. Robben Island prison was shut down. In the 1994 general election, South Africans elected former Robben

Island prisoner Nelson Mandela as their president. Black people were now in power. Among the many changes introduced, the country adopted a new coat of arms that included images of the original inhabitants of South Africa, the San people.

Many former inmates of Robben Island joined the new government, including several Makana veterans. Never before has an amateur football league ended up having such an influential role in the government of a nation. Two Makana players, Kgalema Motlanthe and Jacob Zuma, even became South African presidents! Football gave the Robben Island prisoners a sense of shared purpose, and fostered a love of sport, that continued when they were running the country. The story of the Makana FA shows how football can help those in the bleakest of situations, and is a lesson that we should never stop hoping that the world can change for the better.

STAR UNABLE TO PLAY, OR EVEN WATCH

Nelson Mandela, the figurehead of the anti-racism struggle in South Africa, was imprisoned for 27 years for campaigning against the government, spending eighteen of them on Robben Island. He did not play football in prison because he was kept in solitary confinement. When guards realized he could see the football pitch from his window, they built a wall to stop him watching.

MANCHESTER CITY

Nickname: The Cityzens

Best of the crest:

The ship represents the Manchester Ship Canal, which links the city to the Irish Sea. The red rose is the symbol of Lancashire.

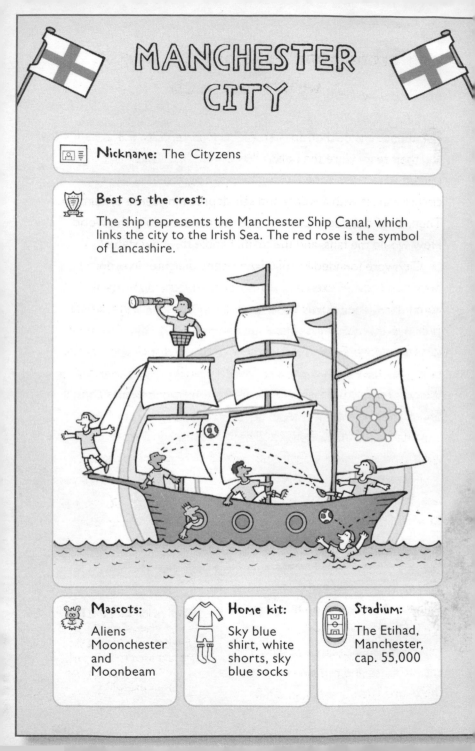

Mascots:

Aliens Moonchester and Moonbeam

Home kit:

Sky blue shirt, white shorts, sky blue socks

Stadium:

The Etihad, Manchester, cap. 55,000

From poor relations to world's wealthiest club

Patience has paid off for fans of Manchester City. For decades their team were the poor relations of local rivals Manchester United. Their fans coped with disappointing results and tragic circumstances with a weary and self-deprecating sense of humour. Then, all of a sudden, City became the richest club in the world. How would the fans, and the team, handle this new status?

City were founded in 1880 by a vicar's daughter in order to provide a form of exercise for poorer members of the local community. They slowly established a reputation as a grassroots club with solid local support. After the Second World War, their local rivals Manchester United became the biggest club in England, with a fan base all over the country. For decades, City resented their more successful neighbours, and misfortune became part of their own club identity.

It was typical of City that they once managed to score more goals than any other team in the division but still got relegated!

It was typical of City that they once played for a draw on the last day of the season when they needed to win to avoid relegation. The manager had mistakenly given them the wrong instructions!

It was typical of City that the club was once better known for fans waving inflatable bananas at matches than for their results on the pitch.

Through it all, however, the fans celebrated their catalogue of catastrophes and remained loyal to the team. Then one day, in 2008,

PHIL YOUR BOOTS

Gifted midfielder Phil Foden joined Manchester City's academy aged four years old and used to be a ballboy at City's home games. Talk about on the ball!

the club's fortunes (and fortune!) changed. A company owned by a member of the Abu Dhabi royal family, one of the richest families in the world, bought the club. City went from the verge of bankruptcy to being the richest football club in the world. In the following years they spent more than £1 billion on players. Yes, you read that correctly: £1 billion.

And it paid dividends. On the final day of the season in 2012, three years after the new owners took over, City had a chance to win their first ever Premier League title. With one match to go, they were leading the table on goal difference over Manchester United. In other words, all City needed to do was equal United's result and they would be champions.

That day has gone down as the most exciting finale in Premier League history. City faced QPR and United faced Sunderland. At half-time both Manchester teams were winning 1–0, meaning that City were on course for the title. But in the second half, City conceded two, and with 90 minutes on the clock were losing 2–1, putting United ahead of them in the table. The whistle went at United's game: they had beaten Sunderland. The United players stayed on the pitch, believing that surely the title was theirs. Was this going to be another example of City snatching defeat from the jaws of victory?

In injury time, however, City striker Edin Džeko headed in an equalizer. There was another 90 seconds to push for a winner. The ball fell to Sergio Agüero, their centre-forward, inside the area. The Argentine smashed the ball into the net. The clock showed 93 minutes and 20 seconds had been played. City had finally done it – just in time! The title was theirs and, with extra sweetness, it was not United's!

City achieved further success after hiring Pep Guardiola as coach in 2016. Guardiola had proven himself to be a tactical mastermind at previous clubs Barcelona and Bayern Munich. He helped City win the Premier League in both 2018 (when they became the first team to reach 100 points in a single season) and 2019.

City fans have now become more used to winning than losing, which has transformed the character of the club. But as we write this, City haven't yet won a European trophy in the first twelve years under their new owners, so fans have also realized that having money doesn't guarantee success. And that's something we can all learn from!

MANCHESTER UNITED

Nickname: The Red Devils

Best of the crest:

The ship represents the Manchester Ship Canal, which links the city to the Irish Sea. The devil was added in 1970 after coach Matt Busby decided the club should be known as the Red Devils.

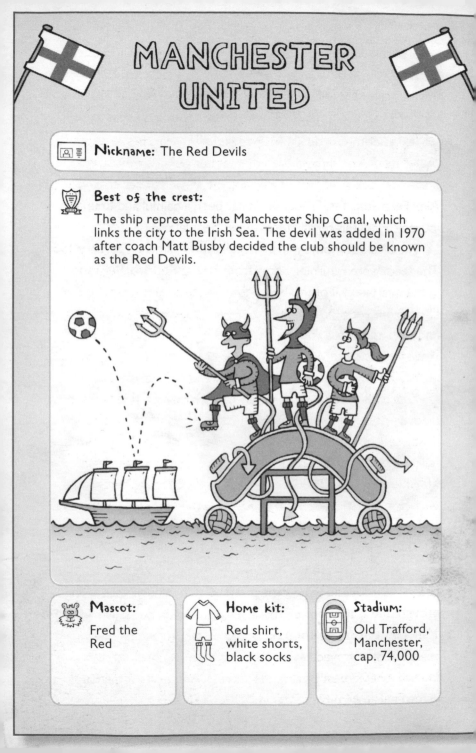

Mascot:

Fred the Red

Home kit:

Red shirt, white shorts, black socks

Stadium:

Old Trafford, Manchester, cap. 74,000

From tragedy to the world's most-loved team

One of the world's most popular sides, Manchester United have lived through two memorable periods of success: the first under coach Sir Matt Busby and the second under coach Sir Alex Ferguson. Yes, Sir-ee! But it has been a painful and dramatic journey. Man, this terrific team unites people!

The bleakest moment in United's history came in February 1958. The team were returning home from playing Red Star Belgrade in the quarter-final of the European Cup, the predecessor of the Champions League. Their plane stopped to refuel at Munich airport and then attempted to take off. At the third attempt, it burst through the end of the runway, crashed into a house and snapped in half. Twenty-three people died, including eight of the players.

Coach Matt Busby was one of the 21 survivors. (He had almost died: a priest twice visited his hospital to read him the last rites.) Busby set about rebuilding the team. He signed Denis Law from Italian side Torino, selected a seventeen-year-old winger from Northern Ireland called George Best, and for captain he chose a goalscoring midfielder, Bobby Charlton, who had escaped the crash with a scratch on his head.

These three players, nicknamed the Holy Trinity, were the beating heart of the United team that brought the team glory at the 1968 European Cup, just ten years after the tragedy at Munich. United beat Benfica 4–1 in the final at Wembley Stadium.

When the final whistle blew, the players had mixed emotions: they were happy to have achieved their dream, but sad for the friends they had lost.

Busby reinvented the role of football manager. He was the first coach to have complete control over player transfers while also taking training sessions. He put his faith in young players and demanded attacking football. The life-affirming story of how a remarkable manager steered a club devastated by loss to champions of Europe turned many people throughout the UK – and all over the world – into Manchester United fans. Since then, United have arguably been the most loved club in the world.

Busby left the club soon after winning the European Cup. There followed a period without success until United appointed a young Scottish coach called Alex Ferguson in 1986. He would go on to have similar success to Busby using the same combination of outstanding leadership skills and a committed group of home-grown players.

But it took time. Ferguson did not do well in his first few seasons: the team finished eleventh twice. It is said that Ferguson would have been sacked if United had lost the 1990 FA Cup final, but they won, beating Crystal Palace after a replay.

That result changed modern football history. Ferguson was allowed more time to build his team and, within a few years, United were dominant again. They won the league title (for the first time since the Busby era) in 1993, and again in 1994. They ended up winning the league an incredible thirteen times over the next 20 seasons.

Like Busby before him, Ferguson was committed to attacking football and developing players from the local area. A group of local lads, who included Paul Scholes and brothers Gary and Phil Neville, were at the heart of Ferguson's Premier-League-winning teams. And, like Busby, Ferguson was desperate to conquer Europe.

His chance came in 1999, when United reached the Champions League final and faced Bayern Munich. With 90 minutes on the clock, Bayern were leading 1–0. But Ferguson's team never gave up. United equalized in injury time and somehow, incredibly, found time to score a winning goal too. They then repeated their victory in 2008, beating Chelsea after a penalty shoot-out.

The players who helped United achieve European success have gone down in history. And everyone still loves the striker who scored that dramatic winning goal against Bayern Munich in 1999.

His name? Ole Gunnar Solskjær. He would go on to manage Manchester United, and on taking the job, admitted that Ferguson remained the biggest influence on his career. That's why his team also has its own core of players from the local area, like Marcus Rashford and Mason Greenwood. United's history-makers will always be united.

RASHFORD IN A RUSH

Marcus Rashford scored two goals in his first match for United, and in his second match too. He was only 18 at the time. Marcus quickly made his mark!

MOUNTAIN OF FIRE AND MIRACLES

Nickname: Olukoya Boys

Best of the crest:

The praying hands on the badge are a reminder of the church that founded and owns the club.

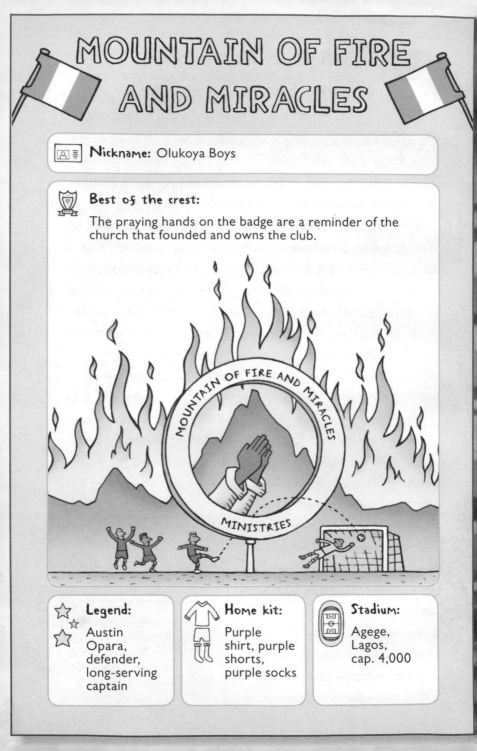

Legend:
Austin Opara, defender, long-serving captain

Home kit:
Purple shirt, purple shorts, purple socks

Stadium:
Agege, Lagos, cap. 4,000

Nigerian church team causing football fireworks

Many top football clubs – including Everton, Manchester City and Celtic – were originally founded by churches, but no church club has had quite as spectacular a rise as Mountain of Fire and Miracles (MFM) FC. Hallelujah!

MFM are based in Lagos, Nigeria, which is the largest city in Africa with a population of almost 24 million people. Yet in 2007, this megacity didn't have a football club that played in the top division of the Nigerian league. Daniel Olukoya, the leader of a group of churches called Mountain of Fire and Miracles Ministries, decided to start an amateur team, with the hope that they would grow and become the best in the city. His plan worked. Within seven years, MFM had made it to the top tier. Fire and miracles indeed!

Mountain of Fire and Miracles is a type of Christian church where the services are full of sound and energy. Believers often go into trance-like states, declaring that God is inside them or shouting to get rid of evil spirits. The church grew out of a prayer group that Olukoya held at his Lagos home in 1989, at which the people who attended reportedly experienced miracles. There were stories of blind people who recovered their sight and others who regained the ability to walk. Word got around and Olukoya was able to expand the prayer group into a network of churches across Nigeria. The estimated number of followers is now more than a million people.

AFRICAN GIANTS

Nigeria have qualified for the World Cup six times, making them the African team with the second-most appearances after neighbours Cameroon.

Olukoya had been a football fan since he was a boy, supporting the local Lagos team and helping out as kit-man for his dad's weekend side. When he set up MFM FC, his aim was twofold: to inspire Lagos's young people, but also to bring more people to his church. He achieved both. In the club's early days, the church helped the football team by scouting players from its members and filling the stands at away matches with MFM followers from the cities they were playing in.

Religion is very present on match days. Before each game, a pastor visits the dressing room to bless the team. The players all get on their knees, hold their palms to the sky and in a trance give themselves to God to ensure victory. Everywhere that MFM go, a band is in the stands playing gospel songs.

MFM entered an amateur league in 2011. In 2013, they won a place in the second tier of the Nigerian league. And in 2015, they were promoted to the Nigerian Professional Football League, the top tier. They avoided relegation in their first season, surviving thanks to goal difference and a saved penalty in the final game. In 2017, they were second – only four points behind the champions, which qualified them for the African Champions League.

One of the reasons for MFM's success was consistency. They kept the same coach, Fidelis Ilechukwu, the same captain, Austin Opara, and the majority of the same team from their journey as amateurs into the top flight. They also took care of the players as though they were family, as long as they stuck to the rules of the club. As a church team, MFM have strict rules about good behaviour!

1. No long hair
2. No obvious tattoos
3. No saggy trousers
4. No smoking or drinking
5. No arguing with referees

"You must stick to the rules," warned Director of Sports Godwin Enakhena. "When you are in Rome, you behave like the Romans."

MFM are now one of the best-supported clubs in Nigeria, and a mainstay of the first division. Their fans will keep praying that more success is on its way!

WHAT A CROSS

These football teams were also founded by churches:

CLUB	FOUNDED BY	YEAR FOUNDED
Everton	St Domingo's Methodist Church	1878
Fulham	St Andrew's Church	1879
Manchester City	St Mark's Anglican Church	1880
Southampton	St Mary's Church	1885
Celtic	St Mary's Catholic Church	1887

NACIONAL

Best of the crest:

The letters CNF stand for Club Nacional de Football (National Football Club).

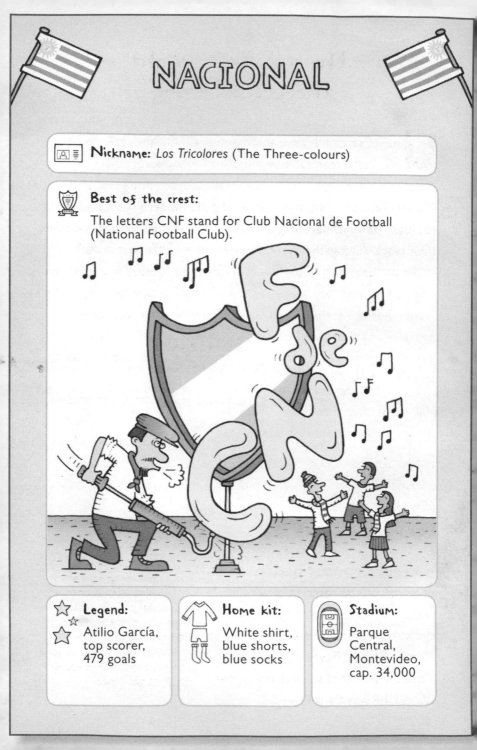

Legend:
Atilio García, top scorer, 479 goals

Home kit:
White shirt, blue shorts, blue socks

Stadium:
Parque Central, Montevideo, cap. 34,000

The club that taught the world to sing

Uruguayan club Nacional are one of South America's most successful teams, having won the Libertadores (the South American equivalent of the Champions League) three times. Nacional are also famous for inventing the modern way of watching football – in which fans sing enthusiastically in the stands to motivate their team. All together now: there's only one Nacionaaaaaal!

At the beginning of the twentieth century, football fans were very different to how they are today. In Uruguay, for example, supporters would dress up in their finest clothes, as though for the opera or theatre, and sit quietly during the games. The only exception would be when a goal was scored, when there was a smattering of applause. Bravo!

One reason for this good behaviour was that the first teams in Uruguay were run by well-to-do British people who had moved there. Most of the players came from the British expatriate community. In 1899, however, a group of Uruguayan students founded Nacional – it means "national" in Spanish – to be a club for all Uruguayans. Nacional were soon to make their noisy mark!

It started in 1905, when the club hired Prudencio Miguel Reyes as *hinchador*, the name given to the person whose job was to pump up the heavy leather footballs before and during matches. Reyes was normally a quiet man, but as soon as the games started, he was transformed.

CRADLE OF TALENT

Many terrific Uruguayan footballers played for Nacional early in their careers, including Diego Godín, the Uruguayan national team's most capped player, and Luis Suárez, its highest goalscorer.

Reyes would run up and down the touchline, shouting encouragement to the players. He started chants of, "Nacional, Nacional, Nacional, let's go, Nacional!" He thought his cheering would give Nacional an advantage and he urged the home fans to join him in his vocal support. At first they were confused but, before too long, they joined in and loudly cheered on the team.

In response, visiting fans sang to support their teams, and would often take songs back to their own stadiums for home matches. They also gave Reyes a nickname, *el hincha*, meaning "the pumper", or "the person who inflates things".

Nacional quickly became famous for having the loudest fans in the country, and the tradition of singing football chants spread across the world. As a result, the word *hincha* became part of football's vocabulary. In the Spanish-speaking world, a *hincha* is a football fanatic.

One reason the behaviour of fans in Uruguay was so influential was that at that time the country was a footballing superpower. Uruguay won the Olympic football gold medal in 1924 and 1928. They also won the first ever World Cup, which was held in Uruguay in 1930. Two of the goals in the final, a 4–2 win over Argentina, were scored by Nacional players.

Nacional are one of the two biggest teams in Uruguay, together with arch-rivals Peñarol. The two clubs have dominated the Uruguayan top flight for more than a century, with more than 100 league titles between them.

Their rivalry is one of the most passionate in the world, and is not just confined to events on the pitch. When Peñarol fans unfurled a flag over 300 metres long during a match in 2011, Nacional fans were determined to outdo them. Two years later they did just that: their flag stretched an incredible 600 metres and won a world record for the longest ever flag.

Today, Nacional are still known for their passionate supporters. For that, they owe a huge debt to Reyes, football's original superfan!

 THE FIRST SOUTH-AMERICAN SUPERSTAR

In 1924, defensive midfielder José Leandro Andrade signed for Nacional. That year, he helped the club win the Uruguayan league, and he also helped his country win their first world title at the Olympic Games in France. Andrade was the sensation of the tournament and became an international celebrity. He was also in the team that won the second Olympic title in 1928 and the World Cup in 1930, making him a triple champion! Andrade was also the first Black man to play an international game in Europe, and the only Black footballer in the Uruguayan team at that time, making him a role model for young Black and mixed-race players.

NAPOLI

Nickname: *Gli Azzurri* (The Blues)

Best of the crest:

The N stands for Napoli, Italian for Naples, a coastal city that looks out onto the Mediterranean sea. The club's blue shirts are inspired by the glistening colour of the water.

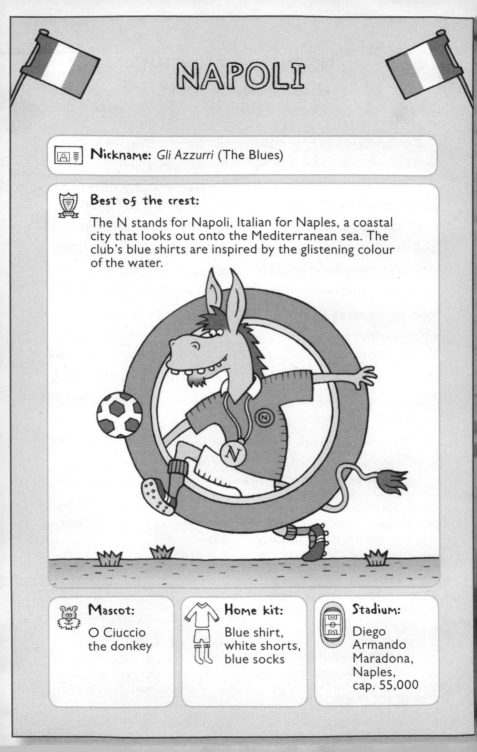

Mascot:

O Ciuccio the donkey

Home kit:

Blue shirt, white shorts, blue socks

Stadium:

Diego Armando Maradona, Naples, cap. 55,000

Maradona the magician makes Italian history

Being a terrific team is about the teamwork, the tactics, the mutual understanding and the unit. But although that's certainly true for most teams, sometimes it is about a single exceptional player! And the best example of how one person lifted an entire team to amazing new heights is when astonishing Argentinian playmaker Diego Maradona transformed lowly Italian club Napoli into double national champions.

Italian football is dominated by clubs from the north of the country, like Juventus in Turin and Internazionale and AC Milan in Milan, partly because the north is much richer than the south. Yet in 1984, Diego Maradona – considered the best player in the world at the time – decided to join Napoli, a club in the southern city of Naples. It was a surprising move for Maradona, who could have had his pick of almost any team. Napoli had just avoided relegation by a single point, and the city of Naples had not only been hit by a recent earthquake but was struggling with unemployment and poverty.

But Maradona and Naples were a perfect match. Maradona was a rebel and liked to fight for the underdog, which is how the people of Naples thought of themselves compared to their richer compatriots in the north. More than 70,000 adoring fans poured into the stadium just to watch him do keepy-uppies on the day he signed. He told them then that he wanted to become their idol as the city reminded him of his hometown, Argentinian capital Buenos Aires. And his wish came true!

THE ENGLISH CONNECTION

English sailor William Poths founded Napoli football club in 1904. Another Englishman, William Garbutt, was appointed coach in 1929.

Over the next seven years, Maradona inspired Napoli to the greatest heights in their history. He proved that one player can push a team to the next level. He was the best dribbler in the world, he scored lots of goals and he made the players around him better. In his first season, he scored such a good free-kick against Juventus that five people watching in the stadium fainted. He was a danger to opponents – and his own fans!

Napoli steadily improved during Maradona's first two years, but the third season was the special one. Napoli went top after beating Juventus 3–1 away from home in game nine, and they stayed there. When they won the league title by three points, it was the first time a team from the south of Italy had become Italian champions. It began a party in Naples that lasted for months: and a generation of babies born that summer were all called Diego! The following season, Napoli were on course to win the league again, but inexplicably lost four of their last five games to just miss out.

By now, Maradona was part of a dangerous strike force, playing just behind Bruno Giordano and Careca, a Brazilian star. Fans took the first two letters of their surnames and together they were known as Ma-Gi-Ca. This trio were magic!

Napoli were on a winning streak: they lifted the UEFA Cup, the forerunner to the Europa League, in 1989 after Maradona inspired them to a dramatic 5–4 win over Stuttgart. In 1990, Napoli won the Italian title again, Maradona becoming top scorer in the league with sixteen goals.

Maradona left Napoli in 1992. The team have not won the league since then, nor have any other from the south of Italy. Yet his legacy remains. After the first title win, giant murals of Maradona appeared on walls throughout the city, and they are still there.

When Maradona died in November 2020, the city went into mourning. The murals became places where people went to grieve. Players wore shirts with pictures of Maradona on the back. Napoli changed its stadium name to Estadio Diego Armando Maradona. He will always be part of the club, with the stadium name a constant reminder of their success together. *Viva, Napoli! Viva, Diego!*

NETHERLANDS

Nickname: *De Oranje* (The Orange)

🛡 **Best of the crest:**

The lion is the national animal of the Netherlands, and the letters KNVB stand for the Koninklijke Nederlandse Voetbalbond, or the Royal Dutch FA.

🏆 **World Cup record:**

Runners-up 1974, 1978 and 2010

👕 **Home kit:**

Orange shirt, orange shorts, orange socks

🏟 **Stadium:**

(Usually) Johan Cruyff Arena, Amsterdam, cap. 56,000

Dutch masters of total football

The Netherlands are a middle-sized European country who have made a massive-sized contribution to world football. In the 1970s, they invented a style of play called total football, a versatile and hard-to-play-against system in which the players swapped positions. One minute a winger was on the wing, the next he was in midfield. Sometimes even the goalkeeper moved up to play in defence! This mixture of adventurousness, adaptability and brilliant technique remains a hallmark of the playing style of the best Dutch footballers today.

The first great achievement of total football came during the 1974 World Cup. The Netherlands, in their first World Cup for 36 years, reached the final, against West Germany. It was one of the most thrilling and nail-biting finals in history. The Dutch scored from the kick-off before their opponents had even touched the ball, but somehow, despite dominating most of the game, the Netherlands ended up losing 2–1. But by losing in such a glorious fashion, the team became more loved, and are now more fondly remembered, than the West Germans who won it. Sometimes you can lose and still be a winner!

The masterminds behind total football were the Netherlands coach Rinus Michels and star player Johan Cruyff. In the early 1970s, Michels coached Ajax, at the time a small club from Amsterdam, to three consecutive European Cups (the predecessor of the Champions League). Cruyff, his star player at Ajax, lit up the 1974 World Cup with his famous "Cruyff turn", a cheeky piece of skill in which he tricked his Swedish opponent about the direction he would move.

The 1974 Netherlands team is considered by football historians to be one of the greatest ever, even though they didn't lift a trophy. The defeat hurt, but it did not change the Dutch philosophy of attacking, adaptable play. It also announced the Netherlands as a major force in world football, a status they retain to this day. The Netherlands reached the World Cup final again in 1978, this time losing to World Cup hosts Argentina.

Meanwhile, Cruyff took the core ideas of total football and introduced them to Barcelona, where he played and then coached. (He taught the style to a generation of talented Barcelona players, like Pep Guardiola and Laurent Blanc, who would go on to become successful coaches using similar ideas.)

Many other Dutch players went on to spread Cruyff's methods, moving to clubs across Europe and using their dazzling originality to mould those teams in their image. This happened at AC Milan in the 1980s with the Dutch trio of Ruud Gullit, Marco van Basten and Frank Rijkaard, Chelsea in the 1990s with Gullit as coach, and Arsenal in the 2000s with Dennis Bergkamp. All were successful thanks to the unique Dutch influence, which combined adventurous attacking tactics with exquisite skills. The national team reached the World Cup final again in 2010 and were at the top of FIFA's rankings for a time.

ZEST IN SHOW

The Netherlands wear orange, but the colour doesn't appear in its national flag. Orange is the traditional colour of the Dutch royal family, the House of Orange-Nassau.

The Netherlands continues to produce more world-class players for their small population than almost any other country. Dutch winger Arjen Robben was at the heart of Bayern Munich's recent success, and defender Virgil van Dijk crucial to Liverpool's triumphs in the 2019 Champions League and 2020 Premier League. Van Dijk's outstanding leadership skills also made him the Netherlands team captain.

Even though the Netherlands have never won a World Cup, they can be proud of all they have achieved in football. In fact, losing in 1974 secured their legacy as the game's great innovators. "Maybe we were the real winners in the end," said Cruyff. "The world remembers our team more."

145

NOTTINGHAM FOREST

 Nickname: The Tricky Trees

Best of the crest:

The tree represents Sherwood Forest, the Nottinghamshire forest where Robin Hood was said to have lived. It is rising out of the River Trent, which flows past the City Ground. The stars represent the two European Cup successes.

Mascot:
Robin Hood

Home kit:
Red shirt, white shorts, red socks

Stadium:
City Ground, West Bridgford, cap. 30,000

Cheeky Cloughie does just enoughie for double Euro glory

Nottinghamshire is famous for a crafty renegade who stole from the rich to give to the poor. No, not Robin Hood – Brian Clough, the eccentric, sharp-tongued coach of Nottingham Forest, whose bargain-basement team twice snatched European silverware.

Nottingham Forest, one of England's oldest clubs, have spent most of their history alternating between the top two tiers. What makes them terrific, however, is their achievements in the late 1970s, when they went from the bottom half of the second division to double European champions in five years. No other team has gone from so low to so high in such a short space of time, and it was largely down to Cloughie, a cheeky chappie and arguably England's finest ever coach.

Clough was a prolific centre-forward, who scored over 200 goals for Middlesbrough before injury ended his playing career. Before he was appointed coach at Forest he had a mixed reputation: he had won the First Division (then the top tier) with Derby County, but had also just left Leeds United after a tempestuous 44 days in charge, during which he had fallen out with many players. When he took over at Forest, they were thirteenth place in the second division and battling to avoid relegation.

His reputation as a straight talker, however, helped win over the Forest players, as did his commitment to playing attacking football. He also had enormous self-confidence.

NOTTS NOT NOTT

Nottingham Forest were founded in 1865, making them England's third-oldest active professional club. And the oldest? Local rivals Notts County, founded in 1862.

Clough inspired total devotion in his team, which helped when it came to his unconventional training methods. Sometimes players would train on the banks of the River Trent; he'd fine anyone who was caught training on a day off; he once made them run bare-legged through stinging nettles. Ouch!

The results proved his methods worked. Forest won promotion to the top flight in Clough's second full season in charge. Just a year later, Forest won the Division One title, an amazing achievement which remains the last time a newly promoted club have become English champions in their first season.

Forest were not a big-money club, but Clough magically turned his squad into an outstanding collective. He kept five of the players from the squad he inherited and added some free transfers and bargain buys. He clinched the signing of defender Larry Lloyd by promising him a new washing machine – and then gave him the one from Forest's laundry room!

The 1978 league title qualified them for the European Cup (the forerunner of the Champions League) where, in the first round, they beat reigning champions Liverpool. In the final, against Swedish side Malmö, star winger John Robertson crossed for striker Trevor Francis, playing in his first European match, to head the only goal of the game. Forest were kings of Europe!

As champions, they qualified for the European Cup the following season. Forest beat Barcelona at Camp Nou and were clapped off the pitch by the Spanish fans. They were back in Spain for the European Cup final, this time against German side Hamburg. Clough had another crazy trick up his sleeve.

He thought the training pitch was too hard so, on the day before the game, he sent goalkeeper Peter Shilton to train on the softest piece of grass he could find: on one of the roundabouts in Madrid's busy city centre. The training session worked; Shilton kept a clean sheet as Forest beat Hamburg 1–0.

After the second European title, Clough stayed at Forest for another thirteen years, retiring when the club were relegated from the Premier League in 1993. The last goal his team scored came from his son Nigel, who went on to become a successful coach himself.

Clough was so popular that he has three statues in his honour: one in his hometown, Middlesbrough, another in Derby, and the third, of course, in Nottingham, where a stand in their stadium and a road leading to it are named after him. What a hat-trick for a coach!

THE WISDOM OF BRIAN CLOUGH

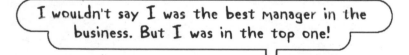

I wouldn't say I was the best manager in the business. But I was in the top one!

We talk about it for twenty minutes and then we decide I was right!

The River Trent is lovely. I know, because I have walked on it for eighteen years.

PARIS SAINT-GERMAIN

🛡 **Best of the crest:**

The Eiffel Tower is Paris's most famous landmark. The fleur-de-lys (a medieval symbol depicting a lily flower) is taken from the crest of the town of Saint-Germain-en-Laye.

Mascot:
Germain the lynx

Home kit:
Blue shirt with red vertical stripe, blue shorts, blue socks

Stadium:
Parc des Princes, Paris, cap. 48,000

Big spenders bring glamour and sparkle to the City of Light

Paris is one of the most glamorous cities in the world, and Paris Saint-Germain is one of the most glamorous football clubs. Yet this wasn't always so. For much of the twentieth century, Paris didn't have a half-decent football team. In 1970, the lack of a big club spurred a group of Parisian businessmen to found PSG by merging two smaller clubs. Their aim was to build a club worthy of the city's size and history. In that they have certainly succeeded!

PSG won their first league title in 1986, and they won again in 1994. Yet it was only when the government of oil-rich Qatar bought the club in 2011 that its fortunes were truly transformed. Qatar provided PSG with an almost unlimited amount of money and, as a result, PSG went on the most lavish spending spree ever seen in football. Well you would, wouldn't you! With money no object, the club bought Brazilian forward Neymar for about £200 million – an absurdly high fee, more than twice the previous transfer world record. Next on the shopping list was eighteen-year-old French forward Kylian Mbappé at £160 million, the world's second-highest transfer, after Neymar, and the highest ever for a teenager. Paris is known as the City of Light. After PSG's cash splurge, it was now the city of football stars!

The Qatari money has led PSG to a near-total domination of the French league, which they won in seven of their first eight seasons in charge.

 LAYE IT ON!

PSG were founded in 1970 when Paris FC merged with Stade Saint-Germain from Saint-Germain-en-Laye, a town (now a suburb) about twelve miles from the centre of Paris.

But what of the attempts to win the ultimate prize – the Champions League, the trophy big clubs cherish most of all and the real purpose of all that cash? Well, it's not been going as well as had been hoped, at least not before this book was printed. Big signing Neymar injured his foot midway through both his first and second seasons, meaning that the player bought to help the team win knockout Champions League games was not able to play when they got to the knockout stages. Oops! In both 2018 and 2019, PSG were eliminated in the round of sixteen. The big-money transfers had not improved the team's chances at all.

Yet, despite the frustrations, the fans were happy enough. Not only were PSG winning the French league every year, but they got to see amazing players every weekend: in particular Neymar, who can turn matches with a single piece of skill, alongside the superfast Mbappé, the France star of the 2018 World Cup. Who wouldn't be overjoyed to see them in their team? PSG's superstars raised the level of French domestic football and increased interest in the French league for all fans.

In 2020, Neymar's third season, they got closer to the Champions League title than ever before. The Brazilian remained free from injury and was crucial in defeating Borussia Dortmund in the round of sixteen, netting goals in both home and away ties. Because of the coronavirus pandemic, the quarter-final was a single game. PSG left it to the last moment to defeat Atalanta 2–1, thanks to a Neymar assist in the ninetieth minute and an Mbappé assist in injury time. For the first time in 25 years, the club were in a Champions League semi-final. *Magnifique!*

In that game, the Parisians made easy work of RB Leipzig, winning 3–0 to put the club in its first ever final, where they faced Bayern Munich. In a close-run match, Bayern won 1–0. After a decade in which PSG had spent about £1 billion on players, they had almost got their hands on the trophy, only to fall short in the final game by the smallest possible margin. *Mon Dieu!*

Will PSG be able to take that final leap and become the first French team to win the Champions League? They have some of the best individual players in the world but, as everyone knows, the best players don't always bring out the best in each other. You need teamwork to be terrific!

PORTLAND TIMBERS

Nickname: The Timbers

Best of the crest:

Portland is a city in the state of Oregon. The state, almost half of which is covered in forest, produces more wood than any other in the USA. TIMBERRRRRRR!!!!

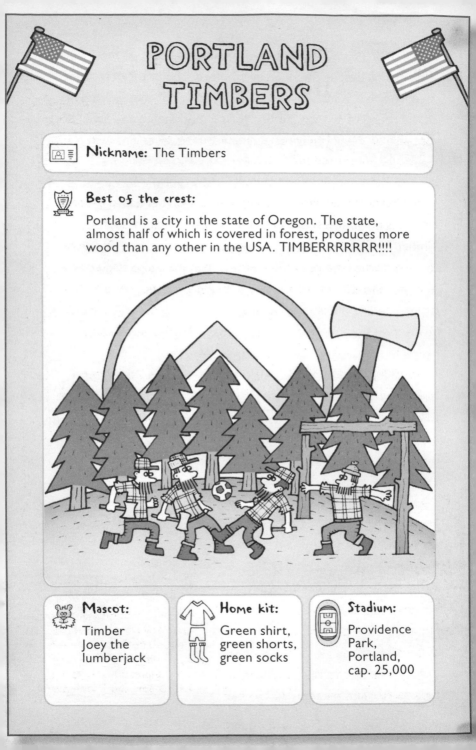

Mascot:
Timber Joey the lumberjack

Home kit:
Green shirt, green shorts, green socks

Stadium:
Providence Park, Portland, cap. 25,000

The fans that see the fan that saws

The Portland Timbers are one of America's best-supported football teams. You could say they have the best team of supporters too!

Jim Serrill would agree. He worked as a lumberjack, a person who cuts down trees, and became the team's first mascot – Timber Jim. Before matches, he would climb up a 24-metre pole to bang a drum and gee up the fans. When the game started, he'd move to the side of the pitch, where there would be a large wooden log resting on its side. Every time Portland scored, he'd cut a slab of the log with a chainsaw. The slabs would be presented to the goalscorers after the game.

In 2004, tragedy struck for Timber Jim, when his daughter Hannah died in a car crash. At the next game, all the fans brought flowers for Jim. This gesture of support and compassion from his community moved him greatly. When Portland scored after 80 minutes, Timber Jim sawed the log as usual, and then he started singing Hannah's favourite song, "You Are My Sunshine".

The fans sang the song back to him and a tradition was born. Jim retired in 2008 and Timber Joey (Joey Webber) took over as team mascot. But to this day, after 80 minutes of every match, the Timbers Army still sing "You Are My Sunshine", whatever the score in the game. For Jim, the song represents happiness, memories and family. Which is exactly what this terrific team and their terrific fans mean to each other.

FAMILY TREE

Portland's women's team, the Thorns, share a stadium with the Timbers. Both teams have the biggest crowds in their leagues. If you support the Timbers, you support the Thorns too!

155

REAL MADRID

Nickname: *Los Merengues* (The Meringues)

Best of the crest:

The interlacing letters MCF denote Madrid Club de Fútbol. The crown was added in 1920 when King Alfonso XIII granted the club royal status.

Legend:
Cristiano Ronaldo, top scorer, 450 goals

Home kit:
White shirt, white shorts, white socks

Stadium:
Santiago Bernabéu, Madrid, cap. 81,000

Marvellous monarchs are the Real deal

Spanish giants Real Madrid are the kings of European football. And it's not just because they have the word *real* – the Spanish word for "royal" – in their name. The club are by far the continent's most successful, having won both the European Cup, which ran from 1955 to 1991, and the Champions League (the successor to the European Cup) more times than anyone else. Majestic Madrid!

The club was originally called plain old Madrid when, in 1920, King Alfonso XIII of Spain gave them permission to add the word "Real". The name turned out to be very appropriate, since in the 1950s Real Madrid invented the idea of "football royalty", with a policy of signing the top players from around the world. The club won the first five editions of the European Cup with an all-star team that included the Argentinian Alfredo Di Stéfano, the Frenchman Raymond Kopa and the Hungarian Ferenc Puskás.

In the 2000s, Real Madrid again filled their team with the world's best footballers. Fans called these players galácticos, meaning galactic people, since they shone even brighter than stars. One of the first galácticos to arrive at Real Madrid was Zinedine Zidane, the French World Cup winner and former FIFA Player of the Year. He joined from Juventus for what was then a world record fee. Zizou, as he was nicknamed, filled his game with tricks and feints and was one of the most watchable players in the world. In his first season, Madrid won the Champions League (for the third time in five years), with Zizou scoring the winning goal in the final, an unstoppable volley from outside the area.

 SWEET!

Madrid are known as *Los Merengues*, or The Meringues, because of their all-white kit.

Back in the days of the European Cup, it was common for clubs to win back-to-back trophies: as well as Madrid, seven other clubs won two or more European Cups in a row. Yet by the time the Champions League started, in 1992, the continent's top clubs were much more equal and for the first 25 years of the competition no club managed to be champions in consecutive years.

Real Madrid became the first – and, as yet, only – team to do so, in 2016, 2017 and 2018. They didn't just win two in a row, they won three! And who was the architect of this performance, which fans called the "three-peat" for repeating three times in a row? Former galáctico Zidane, in his first three years as Real Madrid coach. Three-mendous!

Real Madrid with Zidane as coach were very different to Real Madrid with Zidane as a player. As a coach, he was more interested in the result, no matter how it was achieved. His Real Madrid team were not loved for their style of football, but no one could argue with their results. Or trophies!

His greatest challenge was to build a team spirit within a dressing room made up of superstars, including Cristiano Ronaldo, Gareth Bale and Luka Modrić, each of whom had strong ideas about how the team should play. Captain Sergio Ramos admitted that the dressing room was divided when Zidane first arrived at the club in 2016.

Zidane proved that he knew how to create a team, even if he wasn't the best tactical coach in the world. "Talent alone is not enough," he said. "To win consistently, the dressing room has to be united." Zidane's players were happy and that made all the difference.

Zidane won other trophies during his first three years in charge, including La Liga and the Club World Cup. At the end of these three seasons, he had been in charge for 149 games and won nine trophies – that's a trophy every seventeen games! But one week after the final, to the surprise of everyone, Zidane resigned, saying he thought his players needed a change.

Nine months later, he was persuaded to return as coach, and in 2020 Real Madrid won La Liga again. To manage that despite no longer having all-time leading scorer Cristiano Ronaldo in his side was a spectacular achievement. Zidane, it turns out, is as brilliant as a coach as he was as a player. He has helped Real Madrid keep their position as Europe's most successful team. All hail the Kings!

UNREAL MADRID

The three-in-a-row Champions League finals:

YEAR	OPPONENTS	SCORE
2016	Atlético Madrid	1–1 (Real won 5–3 on penalties)
2017	Juventus	4–1
2018	Liverpool	3–1

SCOTLAND

Best of the crest:

The lion standing on its hind legs with paws raised has been a symbol of Scottish kings for almost a thousand years. The thistle is the national flower of Scotland.

World Cup record:

8 appearances, most recently in 1998

Home kit:

Blue shirt, blue shorts, blue socks

Stadium:

Hampden Park, Glasgow, cap. 52,000

Bravehearts cheered on by fabulous fans

You won't hear this said very often in England, but Scotland were once the best football team in the world. In 1884, Scotland were champions of the first ever international football tournament, a four-team round robin with England, Wales and Ireland. Bonnie Scotland!

Since that magnificent beginning, however, the Scots have never quite fulfilled their potential. They have taken part in eight World Cups, but have never gone beyond the group stage. Their brightest moment was in 1978, when they beat the Netherlands 3–2 in a thrilling match where midfielder Archie Gemmill scored one of the best World Cup goals of all time, beating three players and booting the ball over the keeper.

Despite their lack of silverware, the Scots have contributed to football in other ways. In particular, their fans, the Tartan Army, have an international reputation as the friendliest and funniest in the world. Tartan is part of Scottish national dress. And we mean dress! The Tartan Army wear tartan kilts with their football shirts. They also often wear tartan "See you Jimmy" bunnets, a Scottish type of flat cap. And usually the sound of bagpipes is not far behind! These kilt-wearing superfans certainly know how to put the fun into fitba!

Great Scots!

⚽ UNBE-WEAVE-ABLE!

Tartan is a criss-cross pattern of coloured threads. The Scottish Register of Tartans lists more than 13,000 types. Anyone, from anywhere, can apply to register their own tartan.

SPAIN

🛡 **Best of the crest:**

The columns are the Pillars of Hercules, another name for the headlands at the entrance to the Strait of Gibraltar. Spain's motto, *Plus Ultra*, means "Further Beyond".

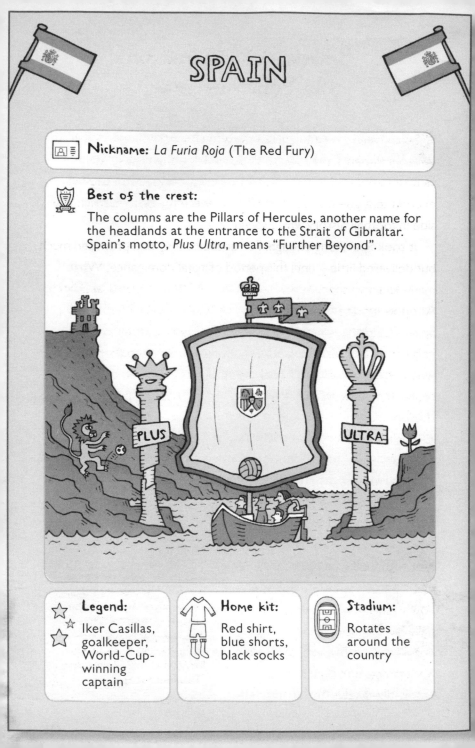

⭐ **Legend:**

Iker Casillas, goalkeeper, World-Cup-winning captain

👕 **Home kit:**

Red shirt, blue shorts, black socks

🏟 **Stadium:**

Rotates around the country

Three in a row for the best team ever!

Spain were the first national team to win three international tournaments in a row. Their deserved – and very different – victories at Euro 2008, the 2010 World Cup and Euro 2012 led experts to argue that this terrific team were the best international side in football history. *Viva España!*

It took Spain long enough. For decades, they had promised much but delivered little – until this period of total dominance. What made Spain so special between 2008 and 2012 was their approach. As opposition teams came up with new strategies to face them, Spain would change their plans to find innovative ways to win. It helped that the team was dominated by players from Barcelona, who played with each other all the time. That allowed their main tactic, known as tiki-taka and based around keeping possession with short passes and fast movement off the ball, to flourish.

Spain won Euro 2008, the first of their three big victories, with an adventurous, attacking team. Inspired by Barcelona midfielder Xavi Hernández, who was voted player of the tournament, they thrashed Russia 3–0 in the semi-final and beat Germany 1–0 in the final. Everyone agreed that the best team had won. More than that, Spanish fans were proud of how the team had played. They believed the intense style of possession, with short passes, was attractive to watch. Fantas-tiki-taka!

RED RAMOS

Spain captain Sergio Ramos is the national team's leading appearance-maker. He also holds the record for the most red cards in La Liga – but has never been sent off for his country. On his best behaviour for Spain!

In the lead up to the 2010 World Cup, Spain had been on an unbeaten run of 35 games. Opponents changed their style in this tournament, though — and in the opening game against Switzerland, Spain were in for a shock. Switzerland defended deep in their own half, with every player behind the ball. There was no room for Xavi or his team-mates to create an opportunity. In fact, Switzerland had one counter-attack and scored to win 1–0. Now the world had seen how mighty Spain could be beaten.

One more defeat would send Spain crashing out of the World Cup. But they did not panic or change their style. As their opponents stayed closer to their own goal, Spain remained patient and trusted in tiki-taka. Spain reached the knockout rounds and beat Portugal, Paraguay and Germany all 1–0. The opposition could never score because they so rarely had the ball. One goal was enough for Spain!

In the final, they were up against the Netherlands, who thought the only way to win was to defend deep and score on the counter-attack. Spain attacked and attacked. The Netherlands defended and defended. For Xavi, it was "a battle to defend the soul of football". Spain kept knocking on the door and the Netherlands kept slamming it shut. Until, late in extra time, Spain midfielder Andrés Iniesta ran onto a loose ball and drilled home a dramatic winner. 1–0 again! This time Spain were champions of the world.

At Euro 2012, Spain were bidding to make history as the first national team to win three tournaments in a row – and the first to successfully defend a European title. Would someone work out a way to beat them this time? Once again, Spain came up with a new solution.

This time, they played without a proper centre-forward. They added an extra midfielder who played as a false nine, a position made successful by Lionel Messi at Barcelona. Messi is from Argentina, so instead Spain used Cesc Fàbregas, who grew up playing for Barcelona and understood the role perfectly.

It may sound strange, but without a centre-forward in their team, Spain were able to create the spaces to score even more goals. In the Euro 2012 final, they blew away in-form Italy, winning 4–0. Once again, possession proved the difference: the final was their tenth knockout match in a row without conceding a goal. And it's not because Spain were a boring side, it's because their opponents could never get the ball!

Uno, dos, tres! Three tournaments and three titles: for this Spain team, good things definitely came in threes! The current crop of Spain players, led by the three-mendous trio Ferran Torres, Pedri and Sergio Reguilón, have the belief that they too can achieve similar success. Three cheers for them!

THE REIGN IN SPAIN

This is how Spain won three tournament finals in a row:

YEAR	TOURNAMENT	OPPONENT	SCORE
2008	Euros	Germany	1–0
2010	World Cup	Netherlands	1–0
2012	Euros	Italy	4–0

ST PAULI

Nickname: *Die Freibeuter der Liga* (The Buccaneers of the League)

Best of the crest:

The castle is a symbol of Hamburg. Most fans, however, use the skull and crossbones, or Jolly Roger, as the club symbol.

Legend:
André Trulsen, defender, most league appearances

Home kit:
Brown shirt, white shorts, brown socks

Stadium:
Millerntor, Hamburg, cap. 30,000

Buccaneers of the Bundesliga

Pirates ahoy! St Pauli are a German club known around the world for flying the skull and crossbones at matches. They also have a politically engaged fan base who support equal rights for people of colour, women and the LGBTQ+ community, and believe in social justice for all.

All football clubs want to win games. St Pauli, however, care just as much about standing up for their beliefs. They were the first club in Germany to introduce a guiding set of principles for how club employees and fans should behave, such as being tolerant and respectful to others and maintaining strong links with their local community.

St Pauli is the name of a neighbourhood in the centre of Hamburg. The area has long been the centre of the city's nightlife, with nightclubs, bars and the biggest funfair in northern Germany. In the 1980s, St Pauli was also home to a vibrant community of young people, rebelling against the traditional way of doing things. They lived for free in empty buildings, played very loud music and did lots of talking about changing the world!

Some of these young people were also fans of St Pauli, and they began to take the Jolly Roger flag to games. A symbol used by pirates, the skull and crossbones is designed to strike fear into whoever sees it. But it also marked out St Pauli's fans as rebels and outsiders, wanting to do things differently.

TASTY TRIVIA

Perhaps the most famous thing to come out of Hamburg is the hamburger, the name for a minced beef patty in bread thought to have originated in the city.

Differently, certainly, to Hamburg, the biggest and most successful football club in the city. In 1983, Hamburg won the European Cup, their highest achievement. But a core group of Hamburg's fans were getting an unpleasant reputation for hooliganism and violence.

In contrast, St Pauli made good behaviour and a commitment to social causes central to what supporting their team was about. This attitude attracted many new fans, and home attendance rose from a couple of thousand to an average of around 30,000. St Pauli became known internationally. Many pop stars around the world, like British rockers Kaiser Chiefs, are fans of St Pauli and its causes.

St Pauli have hosted the FIFI (Federation of International Football Independents) Wild Cup, a world cup for countries not recognised by FIFA, such as Tibet (which is governed by China) and Greenland (which is governed by Denmark). The idea was to give players from these countries a chance to enjoy playing international football.

In 2009, St Pauli enshrined their beliefs into a set of guiding principles. These principles are not about spending the most money, buying the best players or selling the most replica shirts, but about being good citizens. In the world of football, where money dominates, with billionaire owners buying up clubs across Europe, St Pauli fans are proud to be standing up for the little guy.

But what about the football? St Pauli have yo-yoed between the top and second tier of the Bundesliga, where they now reside. Their greatest moment was reaching the semi-final of the German Cup in 2006. They are no match for Bayern Munich, Borussia Dortmund or the other top German clubs.

Yet even so, a recent poll showed that St Pauli are considered the second most likeable club in the country (after Freiburg). As the club like to say: "We don't have silverware. We have a story to tell." Yo, ho, ho, it's a pirate's life for us!

ST PAULI GUIDING PRINCIPLES

Five of the fifteen rules agreed by the club:

1. The club is rooted in a city district and has a responsibility towards the people who live there.
2. The club conveys a way of life, independently of success on the pitch, which is to be nurtured and protected.
3. Tolerance and respect are pillars of the St Pauli philosophy.
4. Adults should not forget they are role models for children and young people.
5. When selling goods or services, the club is not only to be concerned with profit but also with promoting diversity and sustainability.

TORQUAY UNITED

Nickname: The Gulls

Best of the crest:

The arrowhead shapes represent the seagulls that fly over Torquay, a seaside town on the Devon coast.

Mascot:
Gilbert the gull

Home kit:
Yellow shirts, blue shorts, white socks

Stadium:
Plainmoor, Torquay, cap. 6,500

Twist in the tail as dog saves club from relegation

Torquay United are the team that were saved from relegation thanks to an unexpected, four-legged intervention. This story has teeth! A dog ran onto the pitch, took a bite out of a Torquay player – and ended up a hero hound!

On the final day of the 1986–87 season, Torquay were bottom of the Fourth Division (the equivalent of League Two now), facing the humiliating prospect of being the first ever team to be relegated from the Football League. (Before that year, there was no relegation to lower tiers.) Their final game was a home tie against Crewe Alexandra.

Police lined the side of the pitch, in case of crowd trouble. Seven minutes from time, Torquay centre-half Jim McNichol ran up the wing. One of the police dogs thought McNichol might be about to attack his handler, so the dog, called Bryn, charged onto the pitch and bit the player. Ouch! McNichol was bandaged up. When the game restarted ten minutes later, the other games in the league had all finished. Torquay knew that a single goal would save them from relegation. The psychological advantage of knowing what they had to do in a limited time propelled them forward and Torquay scored in the final minutes of injury time. Thanks to the police pooch, they had pulled off an improbable escape. A fang-tastic result for the Gulls!

SHORE THING

Torquay was once an Olympic venue: it hosted the sailing events during the 1948 London Olympic Games. Sen-sea-tional!

TOTTENHAM HOTSPUR

Nickname: Spurs

Best of the crest:

The cockerel is in honour of Sir Harry Hotspur, a fourteenth-century knight whose family owned land in Tottenham, north London. Sir Harry wore spurs on his boots to make his horse gallop faster. He was also a fan of the (now illegal) sport of cock fighting, in which cockerels wearing miniature spurs attacked each other.

Mascot:
Chirpy the cockerel

Home kit:
White shirt, blue shorts, white socks

Stadium:
Tottenham Hotspur, London, cap. 62,000

London club willing to risk everything for glory

Tottenham Hotspur are the chirpiest club in England – and not just because that's the name of their cockerel mascot! Spurs like to do things with a flourish. The north London club's motto is "To Dare is to Do", and this sets the tone for players and bosses alike. Spurs are a team of risk-takers, glory-hunters and dazzling goalscorers. If you want to get lucky, get clucky!

Current stars such as Harry Kane and Son Heung-Min are the latest in a tradition of spectacular Spurs strikers who have sent fans wild with their fearlessness in attack. When playing for England, Kane won the Golden Boot for top scorer at the 2018 World Cup. The only other Englishman to win the World Cup Golden Boot, Gary Lineker in 1986, also played for Spurs. These cockerels were cocks of the walk!

Club legend Danny Blanchflower famously summarised the Spurs attitude: "The game is about glory," he said. He meant that football is not just about winning, it is about the magnificent moments of high drama that have you on the edge of your seat with excitement. And Spurs have had a few of those!

Blanchflower was captain in 1961, when Spurs last won the league. Yet, as you might expect for a band of courageous thrill-seekers, the club is much better at knockout competitions, where every game is life-or-death: they are eight-time FA Cup champions. Indeed, Spurs often do well when the year ends in a 1: their FA Cup titles include 1901, 1921, 1961, 1981 and 1991 – they definitely are a number 1 club!

Their daring attitude isn't just confined to the pitch. When, about a decade ago, Spurs decided to build a new stadium, it was totally in character that they chose to build something impressive and trendsetting. The club wanted the architects to dare and to do, just like their players! They took many risks with several innovative features. The stadium is clad in glass and metal so that from a distance it looks like a crystal-encrusted bowl. It also has the largest single stand in England, which can hold more than 17,000 people. This stand is particularly steep, meaning that all the fans are close to the pitch and the noise when a goal goes in is EXTREMELY LOUD!

COME ON YOU SPURS!

GOAL!

But the most amazing feature is that the stadium has two pitches in it for two different sports: the grass football pitch splits into three parts, which can be retracted to reveal an artificial-turf American football pitch below for NFL matches. Double the matches, double the crowds – and double the money! Pitchy-switcheroo!

Because the stadium has so many complicated features, it took much longer to build and cost almost twice as much money as Spurs expected. For a moment it looked like the club had overstretched itself. In the summer of 2018, a year before the stadium opened, Spurs made history by becoming the first Premier League team to sign NO players in the transfer window before a new season. The club had nothing left in the bank!

Yet this was another risk that paid off. The 2018–19 season turned out to be one of the club's best ever. At the end of the season, the stadium was finally ready and one of the first matches played there was . . . only the first leg of a Champions League quarter-final! The glory club had a glory match to honour their glorious new stadium. Spurs beat Manchester City 1–0 and, after a thrilling second leg in which City had an injury-time goal disallowed for offside, reached the semi-finals for the first time since 1962. Spurs faced Ajax and the games were even more dramatic! In the second leg they came from 2–0 down at half-time to secure an unlikely 3–2 win thanks to an injury-time goal of their own. This is the nail-biting excitement that the club thrives on.

And what happened in the Champions League final? Spurs lost 2–0 to Liverpool. But do you know what? The fans weren't too upset. They were chirpy! As Blanchflower had told them nearly 60 years earlier, winning is not everything. Dare we say it? (Yes, we do!) Glory and style – that's what's important to Spurs!

CAPTAINS FANTASTIC

In 2021, the Spurs squad included six players who had captained their national teams: England, France, Wales, Belgium, Côte d'Ivoire and South Korea. Armbands ahoy!

TURBINE POTSDAM

Best of the crest:

The eagle, which is the symbol of Germany, represents strength, power, speed and vision.

Mascot:

Turbinchen the bee

Home kit:

Blue shirt, blue shorts, blue socks

Stadium:

Karl-Liebknecht-Stadion, Potsdam, cap. 11,000

Crafty coach turbo-charges team to titles

Terrific Turbine Potsdam are German legends: a small company team who became champions of Europe against the odds, under the guidance of the longest-serving coach in women's football. Never the richest or most glamorous club in Germany, they have thrived by picking international stars, such as 2018 Ballon D'Or winner Ada Hegerberg, at the start of their careers. *Wunderbar!*

The club was founded in 1971, when the local energy company in Potsdam decided to start a women's team. Bosses put an advert for a coach on the staff noticeboard. Bernd Schröder, a retired amateur goalkeeper who had a job at the company, applied even though he had never coached before. He was hired and coached the team in their first match to a 3–0 win. Schröder was hooked! He stayed with the club for 45 years.

Back in 1971, Germany was split into two countries: East Germany and West Germany. Potsdam was in the East and played in the East German league, which they won for the first time in 1981, and again in the two years following that. East Germany was much poorer than West and its communist government had strict rules about what its citizens were allowed to do, including forbidding contact with non-communist countries. This meant that Schröder had to do more than just spotting talent, developing tactics and picking a winning team. He also had to be cunning with his own government!

LOTS OF POTS

The three highest goalscorers in women's Champions League history – Conny Pohlers, Anja Mittag and Ada Hegerberg – all played for Turbine Potsdam. A triple triumph!

For example, East German football teams were only allowed to visit a small list of approved countries, and only play against teams from those countries. In 1983, Potsdam were invited to play in a tournament in Hungary, an approved country, but against some teams from non-approved countries. Schröder asked the Hungarian organisers to change the list of competing teams so it looked like all the teams were approved. Unlucky for Schröder, however, the government found out. In its fury, it banned Schröder from travelling for one year.

After the ban, Potsdam were invited to play in Poland, another approved country. Schröder was desperate for his team to play, and so he pulled the same trick. Except this time, he altered the list of teams himself. When the East German official travelling with the team found out, he withdrew Turbine Potsdam from the tournament and the team were banned from playing any matches abroad again. They were all grounded!

Freedom for the club beckoned when, in 1990, East and West Germany were reunited. With less strict government controls, Potsdam were now allowed to play wherever they wanted. But there were new challenges. Their main sponsor withdrew its financial support and the club had to prove themselves all over again.

With Schröder still in charge, Turbine Potsdam did just that. They started playing in the Frauen-Bundesliga – the women's league for all of Germany – and entered the German Cup for the first time. Schröder's smart eye saw him sign Nadine Angerer and Anja Mittag, fantastic players who would later become crucial members of the Germany team that won the 2003 World Cup.

Potsdam were not the wealthiest club in the Bundesliga, but soon they were the best. In 2004, they won the Bundesliga and the German Cup double. The Cup final was played in Berlin's Olympic stadium in front of 30,000 fans. Potsdam beat Frankfurt 3–0. "That was a breakthrough result for us," Schröder remembers.

The following season, in 2005, they won the UEFA Women's Cup. And in 2010, the year that tournament was renamed the Champions League, they won it a second time, beating Olympique Lyon after a dramatic penalty shoot-out.

Schröder was 73 when he retired as Turbine Potsdam coach in 2016. His team remains the only one from East Germany to have won the Frauen-Bundesliga, which they have now done six times. Competing against clubs with more resources – like Bayern Munich, Wolfsburg and Hoffenheim – Potsdam are still holding their own. Turbine power!

THE UPPIES AND THE DOONIES

Best of the crest:

The crest of Kirkwall, the town in the Orkney Islands where the Ba' game takes place, includes a three-masted ship, a reference to the town's history as an important seaport. The Latin motto reads: "If God is for us".

ST DEUS NOBISCUM

Games:

25 December and 1 January every year

Home kit:

Normal clothes

Stadium:

Town of Kirkwall, pop. 9,000

Ancient rivals who battle in the streets

The Uppies and the Doonies are two terrifically big teams, who play each other on a terrifically big pitch: matches between them are more than 100-a-side and the goals are about half a mile apart!

The sport these two teams play is the Ba' game ("ba'" stands for ball). It is a type of medieval football that has been played for hundreds of years in the town of Kirkwall in the Orkney Islands, Scotland. The Uppies team is made up of people from the part of the town that is "up" from the cathedral, while the Doonies are from the part that is "down" from the cathedral.

The game starts at the cathedral when a leather ball is thrown into a crowd of several hundred Uppies and Doonies. The Doonies aim to get the ball into the sea 500 metres north of the cathedral, while the Uppies must get the ball to a church 500 metres south of the cathedral. There's no referee and there are no other rules.

Sometimes, the game lasts a few minutes, when a player grabs the ball and rushes through the opposition. But usually the game lasts for hours, with the ball hidden in the middle of a massive, slowly-moving scrum that drifts up and down the town. The winning side gets to keep the ball – and has bragging rights until the next game. Not a ba'd way to kick off the New Year!

TOP TAPE TIP

Players in both teams fix their shoes to their trousers using duct tape. Neither Uppie nor Doonie wants their footwear flying offie!

USA WOMEN

Nickname: USWNT (for United States Women's National Team)

Best of the crest:

The stripes come from the flag of the USA, and the four stars are for the four World Cup victories.

Legend:

Abby Wambach, top scorer, 184 goals, captain

Home kit:

White shirt, blue shorts, white socks

Stadium:

Rotates around the country

The stars that earned their World Cup stripes

When it comes to international women's football, USA leads the way. They are the most successful ever national team, having won the World Cup four times and never finished lower than third place. You ain't gettin' these gals off that podium!

On the pitch, USA's tactics are attack, attack and attack. The team is known for pushing forward at all times. With many of the world's best players in the squad, this strategy is used to devastating effect.

The USWNT have also achieved something else: they have turned the USA, where the traditional sports are American football, baseball and basketball, into a nation of football (or "soccer" as they call the sport) lovers. Carli Lloyd, Megan Rapinoe and Alex Morgan – the stars of the 2015 World Cup – are household names. In fact, the 2015 World Cup final, in which USA beat Japan 5–2 (with Lloyd scoring a hat-trick in the first sixteen minutes) is the most watched football match in American history. (No men's match has had such high viewing figues.)

Lloyd, Rapinoe and Morgan were back again in the 2019 World Cup, although this time it was Rapinoe's tournament: in the final, she scored first in the USA's 2–0 defeat of the Netherlands. Now it's down to a new generation, with future super-Stars like Rose Lavelle and Mallory Pugh ready to fly the flag and earn their super-Stripes.

OOSA? WHO, SIR? USA, SIR!

During USA's debut game, which was played in Italy, local fans chanted "Oosa" for USA. The pronunciation caught on! Now the team kicks off every match with the battle cry "Oosa-Oosa-Oosa-Ah!"

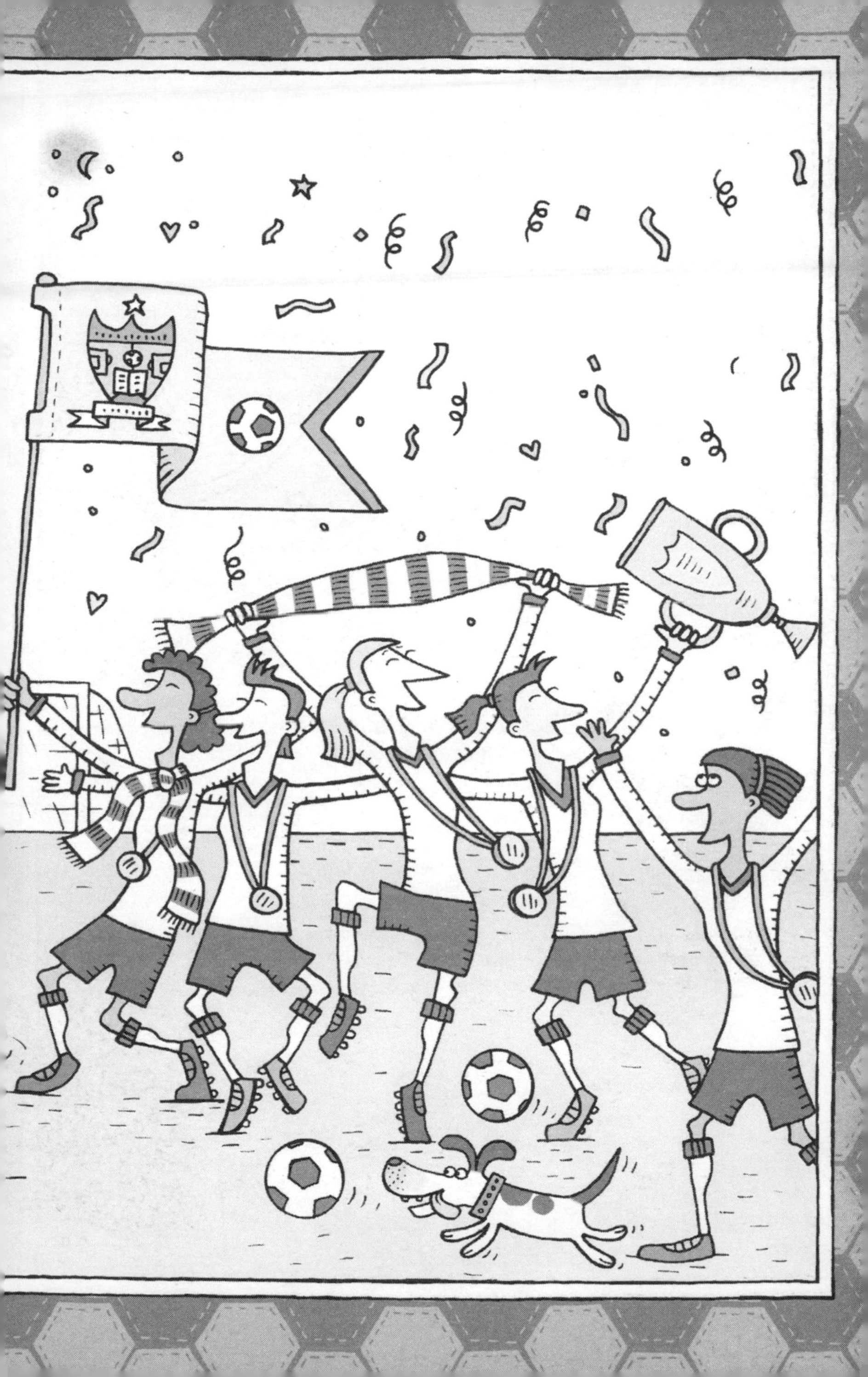

1. **What is Italian for "red", which is one of AC Milan's colours?**

   a) Rosso
   b) Reddio
   c) Rouge
   d) Rojo

2. **Al Ahly have won more trophies than any other club in world football. But what does *Al Ahly* mean in Arabic?**

   a) The Best
   b) The Miracle
   c) The National
   d) Al's Army

3. **What popular Spanish phrase about Alcoyano summed up the club's surprise victory over Real Madrid in 2021?**

   a) More spirit than Alcoyano
   b) The luck of Alcoyano
   c) Alcoyano don't care a cucumber
   d) Alcoyano flipped the tortilla

4. **Against which team did American Samoa end their run of 30 straight losses and win their first match?**

   a) Seychelles
   b) Bahamas
   c) Cuba
   d) Tonga

5. **What was the nickname of the Arsenal team who went unbeaten throughout the 2003–4 season?**

   a) Glory Gunners
   b) Unbeatables
   c) Invincibles
   d) Indestructibles

6. **What record did Arsenal Women set in 2007?**
    a) They went through a whole season without conceding a goal.
    b) They won every match 5–0.
    c) Every player scored at least five goals.
    d) They were the first English women's team to win a European trophy.

7. **What is unique about Athletic Bilbao's approach to picking players?**
    a) They have to be over six feet tall.
    b) They have to speak three languages.
    c) They have to come from the local region.
    d) They have to have red and white striped wallpaper in their bedroom.

8. **Which two animals are on Australia's coat of arms?**
    a) Koala and kookaburra
    b) Kangaroo and emu
    c) Dingo and wombat
    d) Platypus and wallaby

9. **What does the Spanish word *remontada* mean? It's something Barcelona managed against Paris Saint-Germain in the Champions League.**
    a) Double sending off
    b) Goal of the season
    c) Comeback
    d) Hat-trick

10. **What is the name of the Bavarian festival at which Bayern Munich players dress in lederhosen and drink beer?**
    a) Oktoberfest
    b) Beerfest
    c) Bayernfest
    d) Lederfest

11. What is Brazil's footballing claim to fame?

a) They're the only country to have taken part in every World Cup.

b) They've won every World Cup they've played in.

c) They've scored in every World Cup match they've played.

d) They're the most populous country to play in the World Cup.

12. How did Bungay Town make headlines with a match in 2012?

a) The players paid the fans to attend.

b) A dog ran onto the pitch as lightning struck the stadium.

c) The pitch was covered in mushrooms which the players had to eat before kick-off.

d) Everyone on the pitch, including the referee, had the surname Bungay.

13. What record did Cameroon striker Roger Milla break twice in successive World Cups?

a) Best dancer at the World Cup

b) Most substitute appearances at the World Cup

c) Scoring from the furthest distance at the World Cup

d) Oldest goalscorer at the World Cup

14. Why is the job of Chelsea coach a risky one?

a) A tarantula that escaped from a local exotic pet shop lives in the coach's office.

b) They have sacked more coaches than any other Premier League team in the last eighteen years.

c) If the team lose five games, the coach gets thrown off the owner's yacht and has to swim to shore.

d) Every time the team loses, the coach has to sing karaoke on the team bus.

15. What job did Chelsea Women's coach Emma Hayes train for before moving into football?

a) Spy

b) Doctor

c) Taxi driver

d) Lawyer

16. **Which Brazilian team is named after an amateur English side that toured Brazil in 1910?**

   a) Flamengo
   b) Botafogo
   c) Palmeiras
   d) Corinthians

17. **Dick, Kerr Ladies were named after the factory where all the players worked. What did the factory produce?**

   a) Cars
   b) Military equipment and weapons
   c) Football boots
   d) Medicine

18. **What symbol of Yorkshire appears on the crest of the Doncaster Belles?**

   a) Yorkshire pudding
   b) York Castle
   c) White rose
   d) Yorkie bar

19. **What record did Jordan Pickford break when England beat Switzerland in the 2019 UEFA Nations League?**

   a) First England goalkeeper to save five penalties
   b) First England goalkeeper to get sent off during a penalty shoot-out
   c) First England goalkeeper to captain the team
   d) First England goalkeeper to score a penalty

20. **Which two teams beat the England Lionesses in the 2015 and 2019 World Cup semi-finals?**

   a) Japan and USA
   b) Netherlands and Germany
   c) France and Brazil
   d) Canada and Sweden

21. **Which of the following facts about Danish club FC Nordsjælland is true?**

a) They are paid in Danish pastries.

b) Their mascot is a mermaid.

c) Their nickname is the Great Danes.

d) They have the youngest average age of Europe's top tier teams.

22. **Forest Green Rovers owner Dale Vince changed the club's kit to resemble the stripes of which animal?**

a) Tiger

b) Bumblebee

c) Skunk

d) Zebra

23. **Which France striker scored in the 2018 World Cup final, becoming the first teenager to score in the final since Pelé back in 1958?**

a) Antoine Griezmann

b) Kylian Mbappé

c) Olivier Giroud

d) Marcus Thuram

24. **What company did German shoemaker Adi Dassler set up after helping West Germany win the 1954 World Cup final?**

a) Nike

b) Under Armour

c) Puma

d) Adidas

25. **What does the Arabic phrase *Allahu Akbar*, which appears on the Iraq team crest, mean?**

a) Let's win every game!

b) Never give up!

c) God is the greatest!

d) We all love Iraq!

26. **What advice did Dino Zoff take from his grandma to grow in height, before he became Italy's World-Cup-winning goalkeeper? (We don't recommend any of these!)**

   a) Hang by your arms from monkey bars for two hours a day.
   b) Eat eight eggs a day.
   c) Run ten miles a day.
   d) Water your feet.

27. **What is special about the *yatagarasu*, the crow that appears on the Japan Women's team crest?**

   a) It has three legs.
   b) It has two beaks.
   c) It has no feathers.
   d) It has all of the above.

28. **What is Italian club Juventus's nickname? (Clue: *Juventus* means "youth" in Latin.)**

   a) The Young Man
   b) The Old Lady
   c) The Middle-Aged Chap
   d) The Terrific Toddlers

29. **What is Lewes best known for? (Even more than its football club!)**

   a) Beaches
   b) Dinosaur footprints
   c) The local cuisine
   d) Bonfire Night celebrations

30. **What was kept in the storeroom where Liverpool coaches would meet to discuss the tactics that helped them win European trophies?**

   a) Toilet roll
   b) Biscuits
   c) Mops
   d) Boots

31. **Lyon Women broke a record in club football by winning how many matches in a row?**

   a) 26
   b) 34
   c) 41
   d) 53

32. **What important position in South Africa did Jacob Zuma, who played in the Makana FA when he was an inmate of Robben Island prison, occupy many years later?**

   a) Coach of the national team
   b) President
   c) Poet Laureate
   d) Captain of the national team

33. **What inflatable object did Manchester City fans bring to matches to cheer everyone up?**

   a) Beach balls
   b) Crocodiles
   c) Paddling pools
   d) Bananas

34. **Which team did Manchester United beat 4–1 in their first European Cup final win in 1968?**

   a) Benfica
   b) Real Madrid
   c) Bayern Munich
   d) Red Star Belgrade

35. **Which of the following are banned for Mountain of Fire and Miracles FC players?**

   a) New trainers
   b) Bright clothes
   c) Long hair
   d) Smelly socks

36. **What was Prudencio Miguel Reyes' official job at Uruguayan club Nacional? (He was the first person to get fans chanting.)**

a) He pumped up the balls.
b) He was the club chef.
c) He trained the goalkeepers.
d) He ironed the kits.

37. **What inspired the colour of Napoli's blue shirts?**

a) Gorgonzola cheese
b) Vesuvius
c) Blueberry pizza
d) The sea

38. **What was the name given to Johan Cruyff's piece of trickery for the Netherlands when he bamboozled a Swedish defender at the 1974 World Cup?**

a) Cruyff Con
b) Cruyff Deception
c) Cruyff Turn
d) Cruyff Wobble

39. **Where did Nottingham Forest goalkeeper Peter Shilton train before the 1979 European Cup final?**

a) In a car park
b) In the middle of a roundabout
c) In a swimming pool
d) In his hotel room

40. **Which player did Paris Saint-Germain sign for £200 million to break the transfer world record?**

a) Lionel Messi
b) Neymar
c) Kylian Mbappé
d) Erling Haaland

41. The Portland Timbers have a lumberjack as their mascot. What is a lumberjack?

a) A tree

b) Someone who plants trees

c) Someone who cuts down trees

d) A carpenter

42. What food is Real Madrid's nickname because of their all-white kit?

a) The Meringues

b) The Coconuts

c) The Mushrooms

d) The Onions

43. What is the nickname of Scotland fans who make friends when they travel the world supporting the team?

a) The Tartan Army

b) The Scotch Swarm

c) The Highland Horde

d) The Mighty McMob

44. Spain won three international tournaments in a row between 2008 and 2012. Which club side did most of their players come from?

a) Real Madrid

b) Athletic Bilbao

c) Barcelona

d) Manchester City

45. St Pauli fans show their rebel nature by waving flags with what on them?

a) Hamburger and chips

b) Skull and crossbones

c) Eagle and prey

d) Lightning strike

46. What did a police dog do when it disrupted Torquay United's last match of the 1987 season in the final minutes? Fans think this act helped save the club from relegation.

a) Did a poo on the pitch

b) Sniffed the goalkeeper's bum

c) Headed the ball into the goal

d) Bit the leg of a player

47. Where does the "Hotspur" in Tottenham Hotspur come from?

a) Sir Jimmy Hotspur, who coached the club to win their first trophy in 1901

b) Sir Hugo Hotspur, who founded the club in 1882

c) Sir Harry Hotspur, a knight whose family owned land in Tottenham

d) Sir Gareth Hotspur, a famous barber who styled the players in the 1880s

48. Which striker played for Turbine Potsdam early in her career?

a) Pernille Harder

b) Vivianne Miedema

c) Fran Kirby

d) Ada Hegerberg

49. In the Ba' game between the Uppies and the Doonies in Kirkwall, Orkney, where are the Doonies trying to get the ball to?

a) The bingo hall

b) The castle

c) The sea

d) The chip shop

50. What did USA striker Carli Lloyd manage to do in the first sixteen minutes of the 2015 World Cup final against Japan?

a) Score a goal and then get sent off

b) Score a hat-trick

c) Score a goal and then an own goal

d) Score a penalty then miss a penalty

QUIZ ANSWERS

1. a)	**16.** d)
2. c)	**17.** b)
3. a)	**18.** c)
4. d)	**19.** d)
5. c)	**20.** a)
6. d)	**21.** d)
7. c)	**22.** d)
8. b)	**23.** b)
9. c)	**24.** d)
10. a)	**25.** c)
11. a)	**26.** b)
12. d)	**27.** a)
13. d)	**28.** b)
14. b)	**29.** d)
15. a)	**30.** d)

31. c)	**41.** c)
32. b)	**42.** a)
33. d)	**43.** a)
34. a)	**44.** c)
35. c)	**45.** b)
36. a)	**46.** d)
37. d)	**47.** c)
38. c)	**48.** d)
39. b)	**49.** c)
40. b)	**50.** b)

....

Nickname:

Best of the crest:

World Cup record:

Home kit:

Stadium:

....

🪪 **Nickname:**

🛡 **Best of the crest:**

🦔 **Mascot:**

👕 **Home kit:**

🏟 **Stadium:**

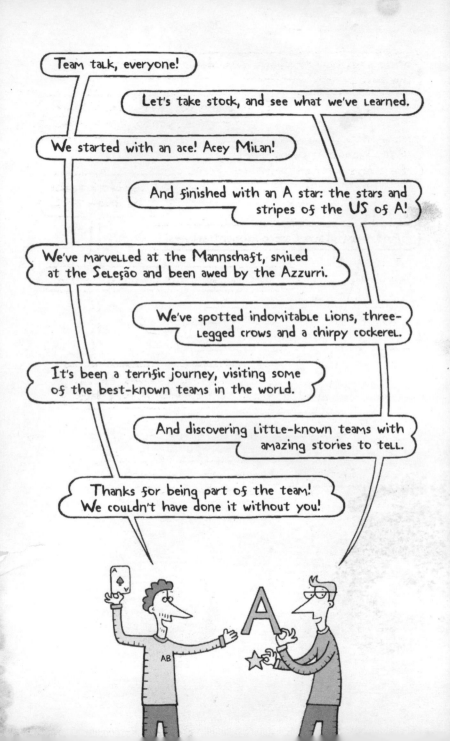

ACKNOWLEDGEMENTS

Football School is privileged to have terrific illustrator Spike Gerrell on its team. This visual virtuoso is a ninja of the nib and a sorcerer of the sketch! His creative crest interpretations creased us up. Bravo Spike!

The teamwork at Walker HQ was tip-top as ever, led by Daisy Jellicoe. Thank you DJ, and good luck with the new member of your team! We also want to thank Ellen Abernathy, Josh Alliston, Laurelie Bazin, Rosi Crawley, Jo Humphreys-Davies, Rebecca Oram, Alice Primmer, Maryam Rimi, Ed Ripley – and of course, team skipper Denise Johnstone-Burt.

Team hugs to our agents Rebecca Carter, Kirsty Gordon, Ellis Hazelgrove, David Luxton, Rebecca Winfield and Nick Walters.

We would also like to thank the following team-mates and friends who helped us along the way: Dominic Bliss, Shaun Cole, Amro Elserty, Gary James, Helen Johnson, James Montague, Maggie Murphy, Tancredi Palmeri, Ignacio Palacios-Huerta, Jack Pitt-Brooke, Raffaele Poli, Paul Saffer, Mick Simpson, Tom Vernon, Dale Vince, John Wasko and Jean Williams.

Finally, Ben would like to thank Annie, Clemmy and Bibi for making the best team ever, and Buddy for his tactical team-talks and training tribulations. Alex would like to thank Nat, Zak, Barnaby, Pinky, Bobo and Omelete.

ABOUT YOUR COACHES

Alex Bellos writes for the *Guardian*. He has written several bestselling popular science books and created two mathematical colouring books. He loves puzzles.

Ben Lyttleton is a journalist, broadcaster and football consultant. He has written books about how to score the perfect penalty and what we can learn from football's best managers.

Spike Gerrell grew up loving both playing football and drawing pictures. He now gets to draw for a living. At heart, though, he will always be a central midfielder.

MORE FROM FOOTBALL SCHOOL

Find out about our amazing world through football

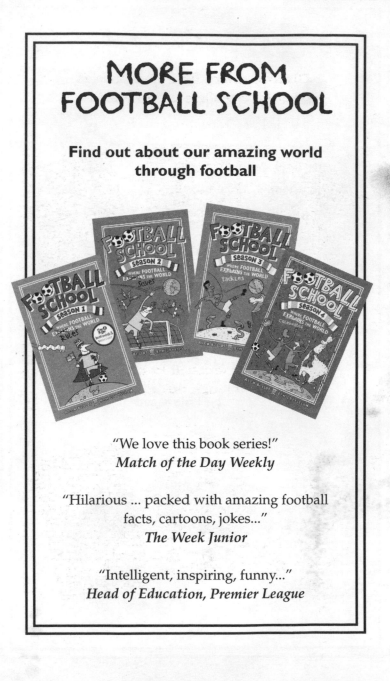

"We love this book series!"
Match of the Day Weekly

"Hilarious ... packed with amazing football facts, cartoons, jokes..."
The Week Junior

"Intelligent, inspiring, funny..."
Head of Education, Premier League

Discover incredible true stories
about top players and teams

Test your football knowledge
and laugh out loud

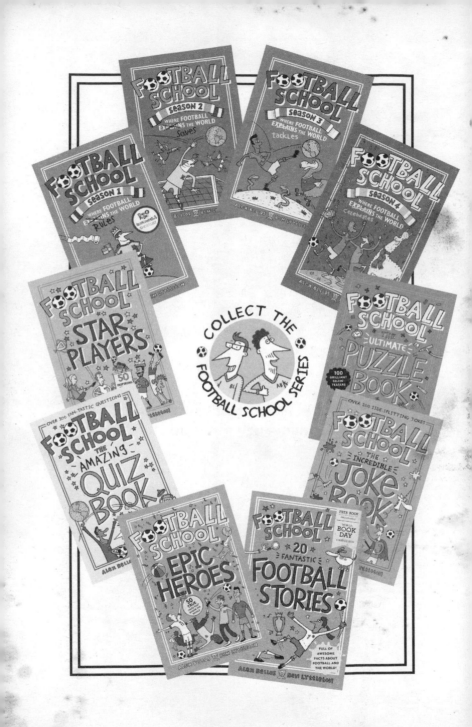